Manifestation of His Presence

SOPHIA GRANT

Manifestation of His Presence

SOPHIA GRANT

Bridge-Logos *Publishers*

Gainesville, Florida 32614 USA

Manifestation of His Presence
by Sophia Grant
Copyright © 2000 by Bridge-Logos Publishers
Library of Congress Catalog Card Number: Pending
International Standard Book Number: 0-88270-805-8

Published by:

Bridge-Logos *Publishers*
PO Box 141630
Gainesville, FL 32614
http://www.bridgelogos.com

Acknowledgments

My Grandmother, Daisy Gibson, for her 100-fold surrender to God.

Brother and Sister Gorman for their love and companionship in my hardest hours.

Charlotte Miller, Sharon Sudderberg, Ervinette Dilger, Liberty Savard and my precious Aunt Jerry Dodson for their standing by me and encouraging me—always directing me into the Scriptures by God's Holy Spirit. Thank you!

Charlotte Potter—every time she opens her lips of clay, God's Spirit pours out like a water fount, pouring healing and deliverance through God's holy Word.

Jonathon Wood, Zane Harp and Patrick Moore for their consistent praying and knowledge that nothing is impossible with God!

There are many good things I could say about the author of the book *Manifestation Of His Presence* but what I wish to say is that after reading this book I was challenged and illuminated by how Sophia was faced with some of life's hardest test and trials and won them.

James S. Barnard

A compilation of delightful, inspiring, uplifting short stories which testify of the "Manifestations of His Presence" in the life of this blessed woman as she faced the "many trials and tribulations of the righteous" with a special childlike faith. This book can be read again and again as a faith builder and is ideal as a daily devotional. If you like personal testimonies, it will be hard to put down.

Kevin Burnor, M.A.
Pastor/Pastoral Counselor

I encourage you to read Sophia's book both thoughtfully and prayerfully. As you do, I am confident that your heart will experience God's awesome love, care and transforming power!

Dr. Kandee Mamula

As a sixteen-year old, I found this book to be inspirational. Mrs. Grant describes many challenging circumstances, yet always held a positive and hopeful outlook. This shows me how God can help with hard times, giving strength to overcome and forgive.

Joshua Radovich

Introduction

When my daughter Kimberly was a little girl, she would stand in front of our house and say, "When I grow up and have a little girl, I'm going to name her Sophia. I can't wait to have a little baby girl and name her Sophia." This was her desire and God gave her the desire of her heart on December 29th, 1992.

It was a really stormy night. My mother was visiting from Oklahoma and we were all in the delivery room with Kimberly when her Sophia was born. Afterward, I had to take my mother to Alta above Auburn to my brother's house. Since it was raining so bad and I could hardly see in front of me as I was driving, my brother suggested that we meet at a half-way point in the small town of Auburn. I agreed and proceeded on up the mountain to Auburn.

On my way back home, I stopped at Charlotte Potter's meeting to pass the "fasting book" around. This is a prayer journal that I have started so that someone is always praying and fasting before God twenty-four hours each day. As the book was circulating, I was sitting in the back row before the service started, feeling completely exhausted. I had been up since early morning and the events of the day had drained me. I was very tired, but I was also very thankful and, as I sat there, I slipped into a deep praise for the safe delivery and for little Sophia. I was so grateful that He had given my daughter and me the desire of our hearts.

As I continued to praise Him, I heard the words, "John 14:21." I softly questioned myself, "John 14:21?" And I heard the same reference again. So I said okay to myself and reached for my Bible. Opening the pages to John 14:21, I began to read: "He that hath my commandments, and keepeth them, he it is that loveth me: and he that loveth me shall be loved of my Father, and I will love him, and will manifest myself to him."

I began to cry and the tears flowed and flowed. How grateful I am that He leads me, He guides me and He's been with me every second of my life. He knows my desires, He knows my cries and He knows my tears and He manifests himself to me.

He does not manifest himself to us because we *have* His commandments. He manifests himself to us when we *do* His commandments. I sat there and cried that night because the name of this book is *The Manifestation of His Presence.*

Manifestation of the Sons of God

For years I thought the name of the book I was writing was going to be "Amazing Grace." However, one morning I was at a Bible study led by the Reverend Al Cardenas, a righteous man of God, who said, "People are looking for the manifestation of His presence." It was like the name was handed to me on a silver platter. My spirit rose inside of me.

Later at a Charlotte Potter meeting, I learned that God was waiting on the manifestation of the sons of God.

For the earnest expectation of the creature
waiteth for the manifestation
of the sons of God.
(Romans 8:19)

Let Not Your Heart Be Troubled

Some think forty is pretty old. Fifty seems even older. But, what about 2,000 years old? That seems inconceivable, doesn't it? In perspective, we're not old at all. Our lives are but flashes of light in the span of history God has given mankind, a span of years that is called "time." As believers, we are but a line in God's great book of life where the names of the redeemed are written.

I remember the early days of my life as a child. Cold Oklahoma days blanketed with snow. I remember many friends and life was light and free. At the age of five, I was both friend and companion to my grandmother who was all alone with no one in her life. No one else, that is, but Jesus. And really, He was her entire life. The two of them, Jesus and my grandmother, welcomed me into their very special relationship.

Supernatural occurrences were every day happenings when I was a child. Many things came our way that others did not understand. We often had no money and no food, yet we never went without. Sometimes things would come in the mail or a neighbor, even strangers just passing by, would stop and want to help.

I see now that this was a special time of learning of the grace and provision of a mighty God who would continue to supernaturally meet my needs throughout my whole life. My grandmother prayed for everything in our lives. I prayed for my mother and father who had gone to California to find work during World War

II. I dearly loved my grandmother, but as is natural with a child, I longed for my mother and father.

Sin came into my life at the age of six. My grandmother led me to the only one who could help me overcome this sin. I overcame sin by giving my life to Jesus. She told me that God's Word said that I was now washed white as snow by Jesus Christ's crimson blood that had been shed for me. That day, when Jesus came into my life, I felt that everything was going to be perfect from then on. I didn't know quite how, but my grandmother said that Christ was now living inside of me, and I believed her.

Neither did I understand that from that day forward, Christ was going to live through me. He was going to use me, as He uses all who love Him and trust in the goodness and mercy of the Father's will, to show His love to the world. I had His promise in the Word that He would never put more upon me than I could bear.

Peace I leave with you,
my peace I give unto you:
not as the world giveth, give I unto you.
Let not your heart be troubled,
neither let it be afraid
(John 14:27)

Fervent Prayer

My mother and father both had sisters and brothers who played a big part in my life. God has sent each one of them to me at special times. I also have many cousins and nieces and nephews chosen by God. Whenever I look at my family, I hear my grandmother's prayers. Each child has my grandmother's spirit within and I know my family is part of the chosen generation.

The effectual (unceasing) fervent prayer
of a righteous man availeth much.
(James 5:16)

Cheerful Giver

My first recollection of being in church and feeling something penetrate my spirit goes back to when I was three years old. I remember being all dressed up and sitting beside my mother on a hard wooden pew. It was my birthday and my parents had given me a black, patent leather purse filled with dimes. This was during the days when a dime would buy two large candy bars. When the offering plate came by, I emptied my purse into the plate.

My mother was very upset with me, but I had an overwhelming feeling of having done exactly what God wanted. I was to learn all through my life that a person can never out-give God.

So let each one give as he purposes in his heart, not grudgingly or of necessity; for God loves a cheerful giver.
(2 Corinthians 9:7 NKJV)

The Hearts of the Children of Men

When I was five years old, my mother and father were in California, working and sending us as much money as possible. I did not understand why things were the way they were and my heart was confused. I longed for the strong, loving arms of my mother. I didn't care about money or their sacrifices to provide for us.

My mother sent me a beautiful doll and my grandmother hung it on the wall where I could only look at it. Oh, how I longed to hold that doll. It was the closest thing I had to having a part of my mother.

The day finally came when my mother and father came home. I was so overjoyed. After the initial greetings were over, my mother saw the doll on the wall and said, "Mother, I wanted Arlene to play with this doll." She took the doll down and handed it to me. At last I had the unattainable doll in my hands.

I turned and ran out of the house to the cellar. Throwing the doll down on the floor of the cellar, I proceeded to stomp on it. I stomped and stomped until the doll was in pieces. I did not understand why it happened or what had triggered the hate that seemed to explode when I finally had the doll in my hands.

I now know that there are different spirits that try to destroy us. There are spirits of hate, abandonment, jealousy and murder, to name a few. As far back as I can remember, these spirits tried to take control of my life.

Hell and destruction are before the Lord: how much more then the hearts of the children of men.
(Proverbs 15:11)

6

Newness of Life

I remember my childhood days as if I had only blinked my eyes. I can still feel that same feeling I had at seven years old—the overwhelming joy I felt after accepting Christ as my personal Savior.

I was convinced that this beautiful feeling would go away from me if I wasn't immediately baptized. Perhaps being separated from my mother and father created the deep need I had to know for a certainty that Jesus would never leave me. Somehow, water baptism became the assurance I felt I could trust that Christ would always be with me.

When I had accepted Jesus into my heart, the minister of our little church said to me, "Arlene, can we wait until next Sunday to baptize you when there will be others to baptize? If you can wait, we won't have to warm up the water twice." A reasonable enough request—unless you were a seven-year old child who felt so compelled to have the assurance of the resurrection through this symbolic watery grave. I quickly replied that I couldn't wait that long, looking anxiously at the minister for a sign that he understood the urgency in my soul.

Something must have touched the pastor's heart because he agreed that he would baptize me that very day. I was baptized and so filled with joy and reassurance that my young soul finally relaxed, comforted that I now had a relationship with Christ that would never be broken. It never has been—I have never known a day since then without Jesus.

*Know ye not, that so many of us
as were baptized into Jesus Christ
were baptized into his death?
Therefore we are buried with him by baptism
unto death:
that like as Christ was raised up from the
dead by the glory of the Father,
even so we also should walk in newness of
life. For if we have been planted together
in the likeness of his death,
we shall also in the likeness of his
resurrection.*

(Romans 6:3-5)

Thou Shalt Not Be Ashamed

When I was in the third grade, I lived with my mother and father and we moved into a house about eight miles from my grandmother's house. One day I came home from school and my mother was crocheting something in variegated shades of pink, like the lacy trim on towels.

I was born on December 8, the number that signifies new beginnings. It was snowing very hard on my birthday that year and my dad, who was a carpenter, was not working because of the weather. On this memorable birthday, my mother surprised me with my favorite breakfast in bed . As she placed the tray in front of me, I was surprised to see a beautiful and familiar doll on the tray beside my plate. The doll had been given to me when I was too little to know how to handle it. When I started to ruin it, my mother wisely set it aside for my future.

The doll stood on a revolving pedestal that played music as she turned around and around. She was wearing a crocheted, variegated pink dress with a black velvet ribbon. I realized my mother had been making the lacy little dress for my birthday doll the whole time that I thought she was making trim for towels.

The breakfast was wonderful, the doll was beautiful and my birthday was perfect. I began to cry and then I sobbed and sobbed. There had been many confusing and troubling circumstances in our home, hard things that I believed were somehow my fault.

But on this day my mother and father made me feel very special and important. They had managed to touch the walls I had built to block out the pain and confusion I felt around me.

Fear not; for thou shalt not be ashamed:
neither be thou confounded (confused);
for thou shalt not be put to shame:
for thou shalt forget the shame of thy youth.
(Isaiah 54:4)

The Lord's Hand is Not Shortened

As my eighth-grade graduation drew near, I frequently admired the ruffled cancan petticoat my mother had bought for me. I would carefully spread it all out so I could admire its beauty, the cancan ruffles almost covering the whole bed. I really loved it.

I was bathing my little sisters in the tub one evening during the week of my eighth-grade graduation when I heard someone pounding urgently on the front door. As I ran to the door, I was startled to see that there were flames everywhere. Then I heard a man's voice yelling, "Lady, your house is on fire. Get out!" I ran back to get the girls, wrapping one in my precious cancan petticoat. Then I hurried out with my sisters.

Once outside, little Neta cried out, "Sweetie pie! Sweetie pie!" Neta had told me one week earlier that she had put her beloved doll "Sweetie pie" in the closet in case the house caught fire. I quickly ran back into the house and went straight to the closet to get "Sweetie pie," Neta's beloved doll.

As soon as I was back outside, I thrust the girls, Neta and Terry, towards a concerned neighbor who was running towards us. I turned and rushed down the street in the direction of my aunt's house, some three blocks away where my mother and father were visiting. I was praying as hard as I could as I ran.

I was surprised when my father's car suddenly raced past me in the direction of our house. I quickly spun around and took out after it. My mother and father had been drinking coffee with my aunt and uncle when they had heard the volunteer firemen's truck head into the neighborhood. My mom said, "Louie, let's go home right now. That's our house that is on fire!" Her spirit was quickened within her that this was what was happening.

When my mother and father jumped out of their car in front of our burning house, our neighbors shouted, "The girls are O.K.!" "But where's my little boy? Where's my little boy?" The neighbors shook their heads. There was no boy!

As I ran back to the house, I heard loud male voices yelling. "You can't go in there, it's too bad. You'll never make it!"

I heard my dad shout, "To hell, I can't—my boy's in there!"

I remember thinking frantically, "They left my brother here? Oh, no, Lord! They never leave my brother when they go out. Please, Lord, let them get my brother out of there!" I had been so excited about my beautiful cancan slip, I hadn't even heard my mother and father say anything about leaving my little brother as they left.

My dad charged past three men and rushed into the burning house. I was praying so hard, my heart hurt and I couldn't breathe. "Please, Lord, let my brother and my father be all right." Finally my father came rushing back out of the flames clutching my little brother, knocking me out of the way as he ran. The smoke was intensely thick and the flames were rampaging.

We all stood together and trembled, frightened and shaken, but our family was intact. God had covered my prayers with mercy and deliverance.

Behold, the Lord's hand is not shortened,
that it cannot save, nor his ear heavy, that it
cannot hear.
(Isaiah 59:1)

Hope and a Future

My baby sister, Sharon, fell off the stairs and landed on her head when she was only eighteen months old and a big bump promptly appeared on her forehead. My Aunt Dorothy, who was caring for her at the time, put ice on the bump and rocked her to sleep.

Back home the next day, little Sharon reached for the phone and my mother said, "No." She reached again for the phone and my mother spoke more firmly, "No, you can't have the phone!" My little sister began to get very upset and started to cry. Then suddenly she was silent and blacked out.

My mother started praying instantly. Then, remembering something my grandmother had told her, she began to breath into Sharon's mouth. Mother stopped only to yell for someone to call the fire department.

When the firemen arrived, two men began working on my little sister. They were unable to get any heart beat or pulse and feared the worst, but my mother kept insisting that they keep trying to revive her. The firemen later said they were thinking to themselves, "We've lost her. She's gone." Finally they placed her into their vehicle and headed for the hospital with the sirens screaming.

The truck raced past my school and I heard the sirens. A strange feeling came over me and suddenly I cried out, "That's my baby sister in there. Oh, God, please save my baby sister." I began to cry as I prayed and prayed. Within a short while, a calm peace fell over me. As soon as school was out, I headed straight for home where I learned of my sister's brush with death.

When the firemen reached the hospital with little Sharon, she was fine. She had received a serious concussion from her earlier fall and deadly pressure had built inside of her head. Undiagnosed by any doctor and unknown by my mother, God had chosen to take care of this pressure which was "miraculously" released when little Sharon blacked out. Once again, God had answered prayer and intervened in a near tragedy.

For I know the plans I have for you; declares the Lord, plans to prosper you and not to harm you, plans to give you hope and a future.
(Jeremiah 29:11 NIV)

No Respecter of Persons

When I was a freshman in junior high school, a tall black girl came up to me one day and stood over me. She said, "Why don't you like me?"

I looked up at her and said, "I like you."

"No, you don't. You're from Oklahoma and they don't like us!"

I instantly knew what she meant. In Oklahoma, blacks were not allowed to live in our neighborhoods, drink from our water fountains, eat in our restaurants or even walk down our streets. I whispered a quick prayer in my heart as she glared at me.

Then I opened my mouth and the words of a little song I had known since I was small came forth from my lips. "I love you. Red or yellow, black or white, they are precious in His sight. Jesus loves the little children of the world." The anger and hurt on her face eased as I spoke that name that always brings healing. From that day forward, she and I were friends.

*Of a truth I perceive
that God is no respecter of persons.*
(Acts 10:34)

A Very Present Help in Trouble!

That same year, in another class, a girl accused me of throwing gum into a girl's hair. I told her that I hadn't done it, but she didn't believe me. This girl was a tall, blonde, white girl who was the leader of a gang of black girls. She looked at me and said, "We'll meet you out front after school," gesturing to the group of black girls standing around her.

I nodded my head in agreement and then began to pray. This time I really beseeched the Lord to intervene on my behalf. "Jesus, Jesus! You are going to have to help me out of this one. I don't know what this is about, but they looked like they wanted to kill me! Please help me, Jesus."

My cousin Jeannie was also in my class and I told her what had happened. After school, she came up to me and said, "Come on, Arlene, let's get out of here and run home before they come."

"I'm going to stay. Jeannie, will you stay here with me?"

"No, I'm going to get Aunt Daisy," she called out as she ran off. Jeannie had unfortunately come down with polio in 1946 before a vaccine was discovered by Dr. Jonas Salk in 1954. Jeannie had just had corrective surgery on her spine and was unable to help me defend myself. She knew that the best thing she could do for me was get Aunt Daisy.

So, Jesus and I went out in front of the school to wait. I was scared. My heart was racing and my stomach was in knots. I prayed and we waited. I prayed some more and waited some more. No one ever showed up and I finally went home.

The next day at school, the same girls now treated me with respect and even affection. Several came up and put their arms around me to ask, "How's it going, Arlene?" Jesus and I had no more trouble with any unfriendly students that year.

> *God is our refuge and strength,*
> *a very present help in trouble.*
> **(Psalm 46:1)**

Blessed Is She Who Has Believed

When I was a sophomore in high school, there were two grocery stores in our neighborhood that were only two blocks apart. We shopped at both stores and every time we shopped at either one, we would get special drawing tickets to win a turkey. It was Thanksgiving and I really wanted those turkeys. I remember how cold it was outside and how badly we needed the food.

My mom and dad were going to Modesto to see my aunt and uncle and I was left to take care of the other children. When they left, my mother said to me, "Arlene, do *not* leave this house!"

"But, Mother, I've got these tickets and they're going to have that drawing for the turkeys. I've been planning on going and I just know we're going to win!"

She replied, "I said, 'Do not leave this house!'" So she walked out and there I was with four little kids— my three sisters and one brother.

After they had left, I started praying, "Lord, I just know I'm going to win those turkeys and we really need the food." So I asked God to take care of everything and take us down there safely and to not let me get in a lot of trouble.

One drawing was going to be at 7:00 p.m. and the other one at 8:00 p.m. I bundled my little sisters and brother into warm coats and went to the 7:00 o'clock drawing. Sure enough, my number was one of those drawn and I won a turkey. I was so excited. We raced home with the turkey and put it in the refrigerator. Then the kids and I ran to the other store.

We were trying to act normal, but we were all excited. By now, the kids believed we were going to win a turkey at the second store, too. This turkey was a live one, complete with all of the fixings. That meant stuffing, pies and (I especially remember) mayonnaise. The food included everything for a Thanksgiving dinner.

The store officials drew my name and I was elated. I don't know if anyone can even imagine how thrilled I was that we were going to get one turkey for Thanksgiving, and God gave us a live turkey so we would be able to have it for Christmas dinner! This was all because of a mighty God who had covered my prayers. I knew that He had covered my prayers and let me win those turkeys because I had been praying so intensely that I would be able to help my mother and father in some way since they were struggling so hard with finances.

How I praised God and how excited we all were. My mother and father were so thrilled that I didn't get into trouble. God thought of everything.

Blessed is she who has believed
that what the Lord has said to her will be
accomplished!
(Luke 1:45, NIV)

You Alone Know Which Way I Ought To Turn

In high school, I had another unusual experience. I was watching the Zane Gray theater on television one night when the host came out on the stage and said, "In the great hands of God I stand." The background went black and all that showed were open hands that were bathed in light reaching towards the viewer. This image penetrated my spirit, and I felt the Spirit of God rise up in me.

I went to my typewriter and typed those words in all caps, "IN THE GREAT HAND OF GOD I STAND." Then I cut out the words and placed them over my picture in my wallet.

The next day as I stood at my locker in physical education, the Dean of Girls came up behind me and said, "Get all of your things out of that locker right now and bring your purse, too. We're going to my office." Shocked, I grabbed my things and hurried to follow her as she marched out of the locker room.

When we got to her office, she began to go through all my things. She looked especially close at my lipsticks. Her face was very hard and her mouth was a thin, angry line. She started going through my wallet. When she saw my picture, she stopped and read, "IN THE GREAT HAND OF GOD I STAND."

Her face softened as she looked at me and said, "You didn't do it!"

"Mrs. Schenk, what was I supposed to have done?" I asked.

"Someone wrote all over the new girls' bathroom walls with lipstick. One of the girls said that she had witnessed you doing it. She's in a lot of trouble. You can go, Arlene." How grateful I was to my Lord that He was in full control of my future as well as my present.

> *For I am overwhelmed and desperate,*
> *and you alone know which way*
> *I ought to turn to miss the traps*
> *my enemies have set for me.*
> **(Psalm 142:3, TLB)**

Commit Your Way to the Lord

My mother had married at age sixteen and had me at seventeen, but my strict father was adamant that no daughter of his would ever date before she was eighteen. I was restricted from almost everything that seemed to swirl around my life except church. So, as I was growing up, I was in church every chance I got, often with my brother and sisters in tow. I was frustrated, but joyful, as I was constantly being exposed to the Word of God and the Christian experience.

Two weeks before my eighteenth birthday, a young man, who often went fishing and frog hunting with my dad, asked if I could go out with him. He said that his mother would be our chaperone. I talked to my dad who swore and said, "No way!" He would not let me date because I wasn't yet eighteen.

Crushed, I watched this tall, handsome, young man move away. He was the type of young man every girl would want to bring home to meet her mama. In fact, my mama knew him and liked him very much. I was convinced that my prince charming had just ridden off over the hill and that I was doomed to be an old maid.

I cried and cried, but tears cleanse the heart and the hurt passed.

On a Sunday afternoon, my friend Janice and I rode our bikes over to a friend's house so she could invite him to attend our church's evening service. Janice and I were the only two girls in this tiny Baptist church of less than half a dozen families. Janice's friend was more interested in watching "Maverick" on television that night, but another youth came walking up.

He was sweaty and covered with dirt and twigs from being unexpectedly pitched off his horse back down the road. Prince Charming he wasn't, but somehow he seemed very innocent and appealing as he stood there looking at us. "How about you?" I was emboldened to ask. "Can you come to church tonight?"

"Will you be there?" he shot back. When I said yes, he replied, "Then I will, too."

This was the beginning of a relationship that would be a big part of my life. Chuck was sixteen years old and I was seventeen. He took me to his junior prom and my senior ball. He also took me to all of his senior football games. He was one of the star players. The Lord didn't leave me out and I was not forgotten.

Commit your way to the LORD,,
Trust also in Him, And He shall bring
it to pass.
(Psalms 37:5, NKJV)

In All Ways, Acknowledge Him

I was chosen queen of our church. All church queens were to attend a city-wide Sweetheart Banquet where one queen of all the Southern Baptist churches in the area would be chosen. I asked Chuck to be my king and he eagerly accepted. I found out later that he had worked for an entire day to buy me a beautiful orchid corsage that I still remember as if I held it in my hands this minute.

Two days before the Sweetheart Banquet, I was called by the tall, handsome boy who had moved from town before my eighteenth birthday—my fantasy Prince Charming! He was in town with his father on a military pick up and wanted me to go out with him the night of the banquet.

My heart started doing flip flops and my mind began to race. Stammering incoherently, I finally got the words out, "I can't. I have this church banquet to go to and I'm the queen."

"Good," he said. "I'll get a tuxedo and I'll be your king."

"But I already promised this other boy that he could be my king."

"Who is he? Do I know him?"

"Yes," I said. "Remember the boy named Chuck?"

"Him? You've got to be kidding!" He began to laugh and say some really unkind things. My fantasy Prince Charming revealed his very ugly feet of clay almost instantly. My Lord, with compassion and grace, opened my eyes that day and caused me to grow up in a matter of minutes.

I went to the banquet and I truly had a ball! Somewhere along the way, I found I had fallen in love with my young banquet king. We had a long courtship—three years of trying, caring and sharing. Having such a long courtship and being a child of God was difficult. But the Lord was living through my life, keeping me holy through the sacred blood of the Lamb.

Trust in the LORD with all your heart,
And lean not on your own understanding;
In all your ways acknowledge Him,
And He shall direct your paths.
(Proverbs 3:5-6, NKJV)

He Will Not Let You Be Tempted

Chuck was saved when he was seventeen years old. Right after he accepted Jesus, he wrote these words on a piece of paper:

If you accept all temptation,
you will forget all salvation.
If you would be on the level,
you can fight against the devil.
Chuck Sheppard

God is faithful; he will not let you be tempted
beyond what you can bear.
(1 Corinthians 10:13, NIV)

For I Have Prayed

I graduated from high school on a Thursday. My dad said, "Hell, you'll never get a job!" I started praying.

On Friday, I went to the telephone company and applied for a job. I took my test, went to work on Monday in the accounting department, and worked there for five years! God listens to our every desire.

Quick, Lord, answer me—for I have prayed.
Listen when I cry to you for help!
(Psalm 141:1, TLB)

How Much More Value Are You?

When I was nineteen, Chuck and I had a serious disagreement and broke off our relationship. Completely devastated, I headed for the park to cry my eyes out. I had been wearing contact lenses for just a short while and the rivers of tears soon washed one of the lenses out of my eye. That just added insult to injury as far as I was concerned, for I had worked very hard to be able to purchase the contacts.

In my emotional state, I concluded that the world had just about ended. Now I didn't have Chuck and I didn't have my contact lens, either.

But the new development was enough to get my attention off crying momentarily, and I began to pray, asking the Lord to help me. I began to crawl around on the grass and search for the tiny piece of plastic, all the while talking to God about my situation. Suddenly a man came up to me and asked, "What are you looking for?" I found it hard to understand him as he had a foreign accent, but I tried to explain.

Then I looked around me for the first time and saw a sea of upturned bottoms. Startled, I realized that there were several people carefully searching in the grass along with me. They had no idea what they were looking for. They simply wanted to help a lady in distress. The sight was so funny, I almost burst out laughing. As I went back to looking, the contact nestled down on a blade of grass right between my hands. I picked it up and jumped to my feet, shouting, "I found it! I found it!" The people around me jumped up and began clapping their hands excitedly.

Later, I wondered where all those people came from? Where did they all suddenly seem to go? Were they angels? And how did I ever find that contact lens in so much grass, especially with only one very blurry contact in my other eye? How wonderful that God cared about something as tiny as my little contact lens.

Consider the ravens,
for they neither sow nor reap,
which have neither storehouse nor barn;
and God feeds them.
Of how much more value are you than the
birds?
(Luke 12:24, NKJV)

Sophía Grant

A Way Which Seemeth Right

One night, when I was nineteen, I drove my 1948 Mercury to a friend's house in an area I did not know. She had given me directions, but they proved to be very difficult to follow. After many wrong turns and hopeless twists, I realized I was headed out of town towards the open country. It was now close to 9:00 o'clock at night.

Turning the car around once again, I suddenly found myself faced with a sign on the side of the road that said DO NOT ENTER. It seemed absurd to me that such a sign was posted right where I wanted to go. I wondered if the sign wasn't just a joke, placed there by some prankster.

It was very dark and secluded in every direction I looked. Frustrated and beginning to worry, I had to make a choice. Should I ignore the sign and drive up onto the well-paved road? ("Probably just a joke, anyway," I told myself again.) Or should I turn around and try to backtrack over the twisting route I had somehow followed to this point?

I decided that didn't appeal to me at all, so I turned onto the roadway and drove past the sign. Almost instantly, several cars were coming straight at me. "Lord, what's happening? What is the matter? Oh, help me, Jesus!" I cried out as I clutched the steering wheel.

It was awful. Cars were swerving to the side of the road, with drivers shaking their fists and blowing their horns. Miraculously, every one of them missed me and no one was hurt.

31

I quickly pulled off to the side of the road and sat there, shaking. I waited until there were no cars coming and then slowly proceeded along the very narrow side of the road. Finally, I realized that there appeared to be more room on the other side of the road and pulled across the double lanes. It was only then that I realized I had been going the wrong way on a freeway.

God heard my prayer on that freeway and saved me from my folly. He also heard every word I prayed as I shakily drove on to find my friend's house. "Where have you been, Arlene?" she asked as she opened the door and saw me standing there.

I stepped inside the door, opened my mouth to reply, and promptly fainted into her boyfriend's arms. As usual, God hadn't let me down for one minute. I promised Him that I would obey all the warning signs and read every map carefully in the future.

> *There is a way which seemeth right unto a man, but the end thereof are the ways of death.*
> **(Proverbs 14:12)**

God Who Shows Mercy

Chuck and I went through several troubled moments during this period of time. He was unsure that I really cared for him because I had never had another boyfriend. So he kept insisting that I date other guys to be sure. I didn't want to date anyone else, so Chuck decided to push me into it. After one particularly bad split between us, Chuck called and asked me to meet him one evening to talk.

I was very excited as I drove to his house to meet him, thinking that surely we could work things out. As I got out of my car, Chuck drove up behind me and began to say terrible, hurtful things to me. I was completely bewildered and shocked as Chuck was usually so kind and gentle. But as he continued to say such awful words, I jumped back in my car and drove away with tears streaming down my face.

My contact lenses began to blur and swim in my eyes and I could barely see the road in front of me, but I wanted to get as far away as I could. I was so emotionally distraught, I was almost completely out of control. All I could think to do was to pray and try to stay on the road.

Suddenly I heard a train whistle scream and I blinked as hard as I could and realized that I was headed straight into the path of a big locomotive. Unable to stop, I twisted the steering wheel as hard as I could and screamed, "God, help me!" My car slid halfway around and the next thing I knew, I was bouncing along beside the speeding train. Finally I managed to stop my car.

Chuck had set me up to try to force me into dating other boys so I would really know if I loved him or not. His insecurity nearly cost me my life, but God was right there once again, saying, "Here I am, Arlene. Cling to me."

> *So then it is not of him who wills,*
> *nor of him who runs,*
> *but of God who shows mercy.*
> **(Romans 9:16, NKJV)**

Whosoever . . . Shall Be Delivered

I once agreed to do a favor for a friend by giving some paperwork to her former husband who was to come by my house. Late that evening, her ex-husband and another man drove up our long driveway. Our house sat back quite a ways from the street behind a garage. Hearing the vehicle in the driveway, I walked outside with the papers.

I was not aware that the man's friend had stepped out of the truck and into the shadow of the garage. As I approached the truck, the second man suddenly came up behind me and pulled me into the truck. Something like a sack was immediately shoved over my head.

I felt the sudden motion of the truck as the ex-husband gunned it back out the driveway and onto the street. I had no idea where we were headed but I started to pray, and asking God for protection and deliverance.

Finally the truck stopped and I was pulled out and led into a house. Inside, the men removed the bag from my head. I stopped praying as I felt the anointing of the Lord come over me and I said with authority and composure, "If you guys have any foul thing on your minds, then you will have to kill me to keep me from making you pay for it. Even if you do kill me, God will still make you pay."

They looked startled and began to talk between themselves in low voices. Glancing frequently at me as they whispered, the men appeared to get more nervous by the minute. I'm not sure what they were seeing in that room with me. Finally they said they were going to take me home, adding, "Hey, no hard feelings, okay?"

I believe the Lord not only gave me the wisdom and courage to face my kidnappers with complete calm, I believe He must have sent a spirit of fear into them.

> *And it shall come to pass, that whosoever shall call on the name of the Lord shall be delivered:*
> *for in mount Zion and in Jerusalem shall be deliverance, as the Lord hath said, and in the remnant whom the Lord shall call.*
> **(Joel 2:32)**

By Their Fruits

When I was twenty, I became friends with June, a young woman with many problems. June could not seem to release her problems to the Jesus I loved, but she was drawn to the love of Jesus in me. She was a chain smoker and nothing I said about the dangers to her health made any difference to her. One day in desperation, as I saw her coming down the hall, I grabbed one of her cigarettes and lit it. When June walked into the room, I put it in my mouth. She grabbed the cigarette out of my mouth and crushed it. Her eyes snapping, she said, "I don't ever want to see you do that again."

"But, June," I said, "is there a difference between you doing it and me doing it?"

"Believe me, Arlene, there's a big difference!" She couldn't seem to tell me what that difference was, but I knew. She could feel Jesus in me.

"Therefore by their fruits
you will know them."
(Matthew 7:20, NKJV)

He Who Has Started A Good Thing

She looked terrible. I'll never forget the sight of June as she walked up my front walkway early on the morning of my 21st birthday. That morning, she was still wearing her party dress and high heels, having partied all the previous night, and was carrying a gigantic picture of Christ. That picture was my birthday present from her. I could see the longing and the pain in her bleary eyes as she gave it to me.

That picture has hung in the entry way of my home ever since. I often think of June when I look at it. It is only a picture, of course. But it does remind those who don't know Jesus that there is something they are missing in their lives.

Whenever you pass in front of the picture, His eyes seem to follow you. I do not know where June is now, but I know that the real Jesus Christ has continued to follow and watch over her. I pray that she has finally been able to receive His love and forgiveness and let Him heal the longing in her heart.

God who began the good work within you
will keep right on helping you grow in his grace
until his task within you is finally finished
on that day when Jesus Christ returns.
(Philippians 1:6, TLB)

About Her Work

Chuck and I were married in his parents' home when I was twenty-one. His mother and father, who accepted Jesus into their hearts one year after their son did, always treated me just like their daughter.

In time, our son was born and we named him after his father. When little Chuckie was fifteen months old, I quit work to stay home with my baby and my husband. I was so excited about having my own home and making it a haven for the two men in my life.

I threw myself into painting the entire inside of the house and my Aunt Dorothy helped me. Every night when Chuck came home, I greeted him in my paint clothes with paint smears from head to foot. He thought that was funny.

She sets about her work vigorously;
her arms are strong for the task.
(Proverbs 31:17, NIV)

Therefore, Choose Life

During the time we were engaged, before our marriage, I asked Chuck to choose between the river rapids and me. Chuck was addicted to riding the rapids of the American River that flowed into Sacramento.

Just one month after I quit my job to stay home, we lost Chuck in a tragic accident on the river. As God said to the Israelites:

I call heaven and earth to record this day against you, that I have set before you
life and death, blessing and cursing:
therefore choose life, that both thou and thy seed may live.
(Deuteronomy 30:19)

Nor His Seed Begging Bread

One month before Chuck's death, he told me that a life insurance man was coming to talk to us. I asked him why he wanted life insurance as he was so young. He only replied that he just wanted to see what the salesman had to say. After listening carefully, Chuck insisted that we take out a policy on his life.

After the insurance man left, Chuck put his arm around me and said, "This is for my baby and my little boy when I'm not here, because I love you guys so much."

The cancelled check for the policy came in the bank statement after he died.

Yet have I not seen the righteous forsaken,
nor his seed begging bread.
(Psalm 37:25b)

The Strength of My Heart

I remember standing and looking out Chuck's mother's kitchen window the day before his death. I told her that I didn't know what I would do if I ever lost Chuck, because I loved him so much.

When I did lose him, I felt that I had a very heavy cross to bear. I did not know how heavy that cross would get.

> *My flesh and my heart faileth:*
> *but God is the strength of my heart,*
> *and my portion for ever.*
> **(Psalm 73:26)**

The Lord Determines His Steps

Prior to the accident, I sensed that God was about to change our lives and I prayed constantly for Chuck. Just one week before the accident, Chuck asked me, "Who do you love the most? Me or God?"

I replied, "Chuck, I love God more than any man. Then I love you."

Prior to our wedding, I had three intense dreams that people would literally have to shake me out of to bring me to consciousness. In every dream, Chuck was hit in the head and died.

In each dream, I told my mama, "Chuck's gone."

She replied, "Chuck who?"

"My Chuck," I said.

I told Chuck about these dreams and he thought they were very funny. He enjoyed telling others about Arlene's "dreams" and would have a good laugh over them. When we laugh at serious things, it is because we don't want to cry.

After our marriage, Chuck had kept his promise to me, never to ride the rapids again. But on that final Sunday, Chuck said that he was going to ride down the ripples in a canoe. Two other couples, family members, went with us to the river. As we were driving there, Chuck said something very strange, "Now Arlene can have her little girl." Chuck had always said that he only wanted one child so we could give that child everything.

As the other wives sat on the bank of the river, laughing and enjoying themselves, I walked the bank of the river and prayed, sensing that something was terribly wrong. Neither the other wives, nor I, were aware that the three men had gone on down the river to the rapids.

Chuck knew in advance that he was going to break his vow that he wouldn't ride the rapids. Before the men left in their canoe, he walked back to kiss me goodbye three separate times. Only two husbands returned to our family that day. Chuck's body wasn't found until two weeks later, but I knew he was dead. When I finally got home from the river that day, I told my mama, "Chuck's dead."

Exactly as she had done in the dream, Mama said, "Chuck who?"

I replied, "My Chuck."

In his heart a man plans his course,
but the Lord determines his steps.
(Proverbs 16:9, NIV)

He Fashioneth Their Hearts

After Chuck's death, my former employer at the telephone company called and asked if I would like to return to work as a supervisor. I had always worked, but I told them no, feeling I had to stay home with my son Chuckie.

If I hadn't had the income from Chuck's life insurance, I would have never been able to make the decision I did. I knew that it was what God wanted me to do. I did not know what the future held, but God knew I only had eight more precious years with Chuckie.

He fashioneth their hearts alike;
he considereth all their works.
(Psalm 33:15)

Set Your Affection on Things Above

While buying a black dress for Chuck's funeral, my mother met another woman who was accompanying her daughter for the same purpose. This young woman had lost her husband in a boating accident the day they found Chuck's body. We hardly spoke to each other at the time, but we recognized each other's pain.

Six months later, I met this young woman again. We were as different as night and day as she lived a lifestyle that I had never known. There was something warm and precious inside of all the pain she had, and I wanted to be her friend. Sometimes I wanted to reach out to her, and other times I wanted to run from her as fast as I could.

I did not know that she would eventually have quite an influence on my future. Today, 35 years later, I still have a very warm spot in my heart for her.

Set your affection on things above,
not on things on the earth.
(Colossians 3:2)

Not Against Flesh and Blood

Chuck was dead. I had finally stopped denying this reality and I knew it was a cross I had to bear. But I kept praying, "Lord, please let me see him again. Bring him to me in a dream." One night I was sound asleep, and I was awakened by a sound. I had been struggling with sleeping ever since Chuck's death as I had never been alone in a house before.

I raised up to look into the darkness of my bedroom and I saw a big man at the foot of my bed. He had on brightly colored clothes, orange, green and gold. In fact, he almost looked like an oversized leprechaun. I immediately sensed this was an evil spirit trying to manifest deep fear in me. With amazing control and authority in my voice and no fear at all, I said, "What in the name of the Lord do you want?"

I turned to rise out of my bed and when I turned back, he was gone. I knew I had seen a spirit from the other realm, but by the power of His Word hidden in me, I had spoken and released God's virtue. His name is wonderful. His name is Jesus!

For we wrestle not against flesh and blood, but against principalities, against powers, against the rulers of the darkness of this world, against wickedness in high places.
(Ephesians 6:12)

Whatsoever You Desire, When You Pray

I wore black and was in mourning for a year following Chuck's death. I simply could not seem to release my loss to the Lord. Instead, I kept begging God to let me dream of Chuck. "Please, Lord," I would cry, "Let me see him one more time." Finally, I did have a dream about Chuck.

In this dream, I was a very young girl again and back in the third grade in Oklahoma. My dad, a very good carpenter, built us a little house on an acre of land about half an acre away from where my grandfather (my father's father) lived in a trailer. There were tall weeds on this acreage with a well-worn trail right through the middle of them between our house and my grandfather's trailer.

In this dream, as a small third-grader, I was lying on the ground on my stomach, looking down this trail. Then I stood to my feet and I began to grow. I grew and grew until I was my full adult size as a woman. As I looked back down the trail, it began to split open in front of me with stairs going down into a dark hole and then back up to the other side where the trail continued on. I began to walk down these stairs and then I saw Chuck on the other side of the stairs.

He had his work clothes on, and was holding a two-by-four on his shoulder with a nail bag on his waist. He was in the middle of the stairs on the other side. I called out, "Chuck, wait for me. Wait a minute, please."

He turned his head to look at me and said, "Don't

worry about me anymore, Arlene."

"No, Chuck, please wait for me. Please." I could not get across to him and I desperately wanted him to stop and wait for me. I called out again, "Wait, please wait."

"No, Arlene, I have work to do," he replied. "Don't worry about me anymore." Then I saw him step on some clouds and onto a glassy, transparent kind of gold street, like ice that you could see through. Suddenly I knew that I had to let him go. He couldn't come back to me and I couldn't go to him. And like he said, he had work to do. I finally released my loss to Jesus and the healing began.

> *Therefore I say unto you,*
> *What things soever, ye desire,*
> *when ye pray, believe that ye receive them.*
> *Ye shall have them.*
> **(Mark 11:24)**

> *And the street of the city was pure gold,*
> *as it were transparent glass.*
> **(Revelation 21:21b)**

I Will Turn Their Mourning

As I mourned my loss, I cried often. I had no idea just how much until the Lord used my son to show me. My son and I were very close. Chuckie loved the Lord with all his heart, a big heart for such a small boy, a heart filled with compassion.

One day Chuckie came into the house and said, "Mama, my puppy just got run over. But if you won't cry, I won't cry. Okay?"

That was the day I realized that I had to stop crying for Chuck and live for myself and my son. The Lord helped me hold back my tears as I ministered to my son.

For I will turn their mourning into joy, and will comfort them, and make them rejoice from their sorrow.
(Jeremiah 31:13b)

In His Time

After I received my life insurance proceeds from Chuck's death, the first thing I bought was a piano for my "daughter." At that time, I didn't have any daughters, in fact I wasn't even married.

Today I have three beautiful girls, Kimberly, Julie and Tiffany, and they are all gifted in music.

He hath made everything beautiful
in his time.
(Ecclesiastes 3:11a)

Be Not Conformed To The World

I never thought I would be involved with another man after Chuck. I dated on occasion, but no one came anywhere near being able to fill Chuck's shoes. My friend, Linda, decided to fix me up with a blind date named Ken. Double dating, the four of us went out to dinner and then the guys took us to a party—the first party I had ever been to outside of church.

This evening was not successful or enjoyable as a blind date. There was drinking at the party, arguing and name calling from a former girlfriend of Ken's and crossed signals all around.

Before the evening was over, I found myself in a position of having to take a firm stand because of my beliefs and my faith in God. As I firmly told Ken why I believed what I did, he looked at me with respect and said, "Someday, I am going to marry a woman like you."

And be not conformed to this world:
but be ye transformed by the renewing of your mind,
that ye may prove what is that good,
and acceptable, and perfect will of God.
(Romans 12:2)

A Time To Laugh . . . A Time To Dance

Ken had been my first blind date, and now he would be the first man I had asked on a date. I asked him to go to a Sweetheart Banquet. We were going to a restaurant with a church group called the Vanguards. He said "yes."

I had a beautiful new dress—a Kelly green knit with a green satin bow on the front. I even had my high-heeled shoes dyed Kelly green. I have green eyes and I felt truly awesome in this outfit.

One hour before Ken was to arrive, he called and said he was going with some friends to Lodi. Would it be okay—would I mind? I prayed, "Lord, let me say the right thing." I said to Ken, "That's fine. Have fun."

There was silence. Then he said, "You're not mad?"

"No, have fun," I said as casually as I could. But when I hung up the phone, I wanted to cry. I was so humiliated at being turned down. I began to pray and feeling somewhat better. I went on to the banquet alone.

As I arrived at the front door, a couple came up to me and introduced me to a male friend of theirs. When I said hi, he asked, "Are you by yourself?" I replied that I was. He said, "Well, you're not now!"

He bought my ticket and we went into the banquet. I could not believe it— I wasn't alone, I wasn't rejected. Here I was with a nice escort. Then he asked me to dance. I loved moving to music, so I began to dance with him.

The floor was full of people, but like magic, the floor emptied as we danced. I felt like I was dancing magically, all over the floor—just like a feather. I noticed that there was a spotlight even trained on us. My dancing "escort" was an Arthur Murray Dance Studio Instructor. Wow! The Lord had done it again.

A time to weep and a time to laugh,
a time to mourn and a time to dance.
(Ecclesiastes 3:4 KJV)

Whether Thou Shalt Save Thy Husband

I dated Ken knowing we were not walking the same path. I had many danger signs. Because of my unresolved issues from my childhood, I thought I could change him.

Before I agreed to marry Ken, I asked him if he would go to church with me. He looked at me and said, "Yes, I will." I finally agreed to the marriage because I was sure that if Ken would go to church, God would be able to get through to him and we would live happily ever after.

Ken did go to church . . . three times. His words after that were, "I've gone to church with you. I never said how many times I would go."

For what knowest thou, O wife,
whether thou shalt save thy husband?
(1 Corinthians 7:16a)

Be Ye Not Unequally Yoked

Ken did marry a woman exactly like me—ME. I was so excited, for I never thought I would ever marry again. Ken's sister, Sharon, and I went shopping for the wedding and I found a beautiful, off-white linen dress with a lace jacket. I chose a blue veil and matching lace gloves to complete the outfit. It was perfect!

I wanted everything to be perfect, yet there were nagging little thoughts that I kept chasing out of my mind. Deep in my heart, I knew that I was disobeying God by marrying a man who was unsaved.

Ken and I were married while he was in boot camp. Chuckie stayed with my mother and I traveled alone to the base. When Ken and I went to the chapel and talked with the chaplain prior to the wedding, I didn't agree with the chaplain's counseling and a feeling of dissention entered the room.

Increasingly nervous, I went to put on my beautiful wedding outfit and the doors were locked to the office where I was to dress. The chaplain didn't have a key. Ken insisted that I could be married in what I was wearing and I was shocked that he thought I would do that. Thoroughly upset by now, I said I wouldn't go through with the wedding unless I could wear my wedding dress. The tension continued to mount.

Finally, the chaplain was able to get the door open and I went inside and shut the door after me. I sat down on a chair and began to sob. I loved Ken, but everything was wrong. I felt God was trying to get through to me, but I didn't want to hear what He was saying. I finally dressed, pulled myself together and praying as hard as I could, I went outside.

Ken was standing there in uniform and he looked so handsome. For a moment, I was almost able to convince myself that I only had a case of bride's jitters. All of his senior officers were there in uniform, too. Part of me wanted to heed God and run, but I was afraid to make waves. I cried throughout the entire ceremony. I knew I was willfully entering into being unequally yoked. I was going against God.

As I cried hot tears of remorse at disobeying my Lord, I did not know that my tears were playing right into a charade already in progress.

Be ye not unequally yoked together with unbelievers:
for what fellowship hath righteousness with unrighteousness? And what communion hath light with darkness?
(2 Corinthians 6:14)

Let The Little Children Come To Me

Ken loved and accepted Chuckie as his own son. Chuckie loved him and even wrote his name as:

Charles Wayne Sheppard Jr. Grant

Chuckie felt secure in Ken's love.

Let the little children come to me,
and do not hinder them,
for the kingdom of God belongs to such as
these.
I tell you the truth,
anyone who will not receive the kingdom of
God
like a little child will never enter it.
(Mark 10:14-15, NIV)

Delight Thyself In The Lord

After Ken and I were married, I began to long for a daughter. I had my boy and now I wanted to have a girl. When I finally became pregnant, I said to Ken, "If this is a boy, can we keep trying until I have my little girl?"

He looked off into space for a moment and then said, "If we can keep trying until I have my boy!"

I laughed and laughed because I felt so happy inside. I was sure God would give us both our desires. When the time came for my baby to be born, I actually saw my little Kimberly going through the birth canal. I began to call out, "It's a girl! It's a girl!."

In a few moments, the very surprised doctor said, "Yes, it is. But how did you know? That's my line!" God had given me a peek even before the doctor knew.

> *Delight thyself also in the Lord;*
> *and he shall give thee*
> *the desires of thine heart."*
> **(Psalm 37:4)**

For Your Benefit

Just before my first husband Chuck died, he had purchased stock in Winchell's Donuts. He enjoyed being involved in the stock market and believed the stock would help provide for our son and me if anything ever happened to him. When Ken and I married, I shared with him that I still had these shares of stock.

Less than a year later, we were stationed in Fort Riley in Kansas when I got word that the Winchell's Donuts shares had split and the company had merged with Denny's Restaurants. This resulted in our investment value increasing dramatically. Excited, we promptly sold the stocks.

Soon after that, Ken received orders to go to Viet Nam and we were sent back home to Sacramento prior to his leaving the States. Within a very short while, our stock broker called Ken and told him of a stock that could make Ken "rich." The broker was so convinced of this stock's potential, he was investing everything he had in it. Ken was very excited and felt he was about to become a "high roller" overnight. He insisted on investing our entire bankroll on this stock.

I went to sleep that night and dreamed that Ken had purchased these shares of stock. The stock began to perform just as the broker had said it would and then plunged to $1.00 per share. We lost everything we had invested! In the dream, I cried and cried, knowing that we had just lost everything Chuck had envisioned as being a nest egg for me and our son.

When I awoke the next morning, I told Ken of the dream and then said, "Listen, Ken, I think the dream I had last night was a warning from God."

Brushing aside my words, he replied, "Arlene, it's $33.00 a share. I want you to go and purchase that stock."

Ken left to help his dad on a cement job in another area of town. My heart was in turmoil; all I could do was pray. Regardless of how much I prayed, I could not get a release in my spirit. I called Ken's stepmother, Marge, and got the phone number and address. Finally, I got in my car and drove where Ken and his dad were working.

Ken saw me and came to the car with a questioning look on his face. I said, "Ken, please reconsider what I told you. I think that dream was a warning."

Exasperated because I had not already done what he told me to do, Ken again ignored my words, saying, "Arlene, that stock is going to go up and it will only cost us more. Go home and order it!" Seeing that he was determined that I do this and completely unwilling to consider anything else, I left.

I still felt such a pressure inside of me that would not release itself. I stopped at a phone booth and called the lady's house where Ken was working. She got Ken on the line, and he said angrily, "I just had to come into this lady's home with my boots on. What do you want?"

"Ken, I just want you to know that in the dream I cried a river of tears. When this dream comes to pass and we lose everything, I will not cry. I have already cried all I am going to."

He replied, "For the last time, Arlene, buy that stock!"

I finally had a release in my spirit that I had done all I could. I submitted to Ken's wishes and purchased the stock. The shares went up to $35.00 and then started rapidly declining until they reached $1.00—just like in the dream. We still have the documents that show how we lost our entire investment because of not listening to God. The dream had indeed been a divine warning.

Although he would struggle again and again in the years to come with surrendering his own will, from that point on, Ken became more open to hearing God's ways of speaking to His children.

You dreamed of coming events.
He who reveals secrets was speaking to you.
But remember, it's not because I am wiser
than any living person that I know this secret
of your dream, for God showed it to me for
your benefit.
(Daniel 2:29-30, TLB)

Don't weary yourself trying to get rich. Why
waste your time? For riches can disappear as
though they had the wings of a bird!
(Proverbs 23:5,TLB)

A just man falleth seven times, and riseth up
again . . .
(Proverbs 24:16a)

He Delivered Me

Ken was in Vietnam on the Thanksgiving when I was pregnant with Kimberly. Chuckie and I went up to Grass Valley to my mother's house, which required us to drive on a very winding road with a drop off on one side. Before I had gotten out of Sacramento, still on the freeway, I came up behind a big semi and I thought of the movie star who had been decapitated. I said to myself, "I have to slow this buggy down!" I was in a sixty-five mile an hour zone, and I was exceeding it a little bit, so I slowed down.

All of a sudden behind me, two policemen on motorcycles signaled for me to pull over. I asked God, "What did I do? What is wrong?"

One of the policemen came up to me and said, "Lady, do you know what the speed limit is?"

I said, "Yes, sir."

He said, "Well, how come you were going so slow?"

"Sir?" I questioned him.

"You were in the fast lane and you have to go the speed limit in the fast lane."

"Sir, I was going the speed limit." He looked at me, staring deep into my eyes. Then he left and talked to his companion on the other cycle. He came back and started to write me a ticket. I said, "Sir, I was going the speed limit."

He asked for my identification, and proceeded to write me a ticket. When he handed it to me, I said, "Sir, I'll see you in court." I calmly pulled back out

on the freeway and continued on towards Grass Valley.
I did keep wondering what had been going on in those
men's minds.

Later I did go to court about this ticket. When the
judge called for the case, I stood up. Then he called
for the policeman, but the officer had not shown up.
The judge dismissed the case. My God delivered me
from injustice.

I sought the Lord, and he answered me,
he delivered me from all my fears.
Those who look to him are radiant;
their faces are never covered with shame.
(Psalm 34:4-5, NIV)

For He Will Command His Angels Concerning You

I continued on up into the foothills that same day, finally turning off toward my mother's road. It was snowing, but I kept driving and reached the point where the road began to drop off on one side. There was a deep layer of snow already on the road and the snow was still falling. The driving became more and more difficult in my little Volkswagen. I kept thinking about the ticket. When I got to the worst part of the road, I was going around a corner and the car started to slide. Try as I might to steer the car to safety, I lost control of it.

I immediately began to pray and cry for help as my car spun around. I couldn't see anything in any direction because of the snow. I just kept praying, because I knew that drop-off was not far away. If another car had been coming around that same corner, anything could have happened. But I know that God covered my prayer and commanded His angels to watch over me. Chuckie and I and the baby inside of me were safe.

For he will command his angels concerning
you to guard you in all your ways;
they will lift you up in their hands,
so that you will not strike your foot against a
stone.
(Psalm 91:11-12, NIV)

65

Instant In Prayer

Ken and I had been married about six months when we were driving on a winding mountain road surrounded by deep snow. The road was treacherous. Ken's mother was sitting in the front seat with Ken, and we were following the car being driven by his sister Sharon.

The road was narrow and had a sheer cliff which dropped away on one side. As we drove along, Sharon's car had a blow out and went completely out of control. It spun around into the lane near the cliff and headed for the drop-off. The steering wheel was whipping around until Sharon could not even keep her hands on it.

In the natural, nothing could have kept that car from flying over the cliff. Ken's mother screamed, "God! No!" Just before plunging over the edge of the road, Sharon's car jerked and spun back to the side of the road, and stopped.

Rejoicing in hope; patient in tribulation;
continuing instant in prayer.
(Romans 12:12)

For All That Are Oppressed

I had married Ken on March 8, 1968. I was happy to the degree that this was the way life unfolds before us when we walk unevenly yoked. My life was hectic and fast and there was no peace in it. On my birthday, December 8, 1971, I went to the mail box just before midnight and there I found a poem from my brother John. God's peace flowed into me from the poem John had written for me.

My Sister

For you, my sister, I sit and write,
For I'm thinking about you this very night.
I think of you often, my sister dear.
And the past and present and the coming years.

My thoughts are not silent, but are never heard.
I can only write them in funny words.
You are wise, my sister, the wisdom of all.
You have felt God's thunder and hardest rainfall.

You have lost, my sister, many times,
But you have won much more, my sister dear,
For God's rains stopped
And the sky became clear.

You have won, my sister, yes, indeed.
Two handsome sons and my beautiful niece.
You have a husband to provide
And keep you happy.

Yes, my sister, you have won.
I think God's thunder will never again come.

Love, your brother
John

Even as I was living out the results of my
disobedience to God, an unveiling of truth was about
to begin in my life. I had projected the image I wanted
to the world and to my family. From outside
appearances, I was an overcomer, wise and happy. But
in reality, I was what people call a "Great Pretender."
God, however, knew I was denying the oppression I
was under and secretly pretending the depression I felt
was not really there.

The eyes of the Lord are in every place,
beholding the evil and the good.
(Proverbs 15:3)

Bless the Lord, O my soul, and forget not all
his benefits:
Who forgiveth all thine iniquities;
who healeth all thy diseases;
Who redeemeth thy life from destruction;
who crowneth thee with lovingkindness and
tender mercies;
Who satisfieth thy mouth with good things;
so that thy youth is renewed like the eagle's.
The Lord executeth righteousness
and judgment for all that are oppressed.
(Psalm 103:2-6)

Children Are An Heritage Of The Lord

When I went to my first teacher's conference for Chuckie, the teacher looked at me and said, "So . . . *you're* Chuck Sheppard's mother."

Taken back, I gulped and thought, "Oh, my, I didn't expect this." I smiled uncertainly and said, "Yes, I am."

"Well, let me tell you something," she stated firmly. "If the kids don't like Chuckie—" As she paused, my heart sank as only a mother's can. Then she continued, "—it's because they love him! The kids here just love Chuckie. He's everyone's friend and they all take their problems to him. He helps and answers each one."

I realized that she had a tear glistening in her eye as she then said, "In fact, I predict that when Chuck grows up, he will be the president of the United States!"

All I could do was thank a mighty God for giving me such a special young son.

Lo, Children are an heritage of the Lord;
and the fruit of the womb is his reward.
(Psalm 127:3)

Did Not Our Heart Burn?

In 1973, Chuckie said to me, "Mama, I want to be baptized."

"Chuckie, that's a really big step in a person's life. Are you sure you want to do this?"

"Yes, Mama. I was saved today and now I want to be baptized."

I looked at his earnest face and said, "Well, son, when you can answer this question, then you'll know you're really saved. Then you can be baptized. I want you to think about it and not answer right at first. If you were in church and a bunch of men came in with machine guns and said they were going to kill all the Christians, would you stand up or sit down and be quiet? When you can answer this, you will know."

Chuckie immediately replied, "Mama, I know I would stand and be shot if I had to, because Jesus has come into my heart. I know He did because my heart burned like it was on fire. There has to be a God to do that."

There has never been a doubt in my mind that Chuckie had experienced exactly what he said.

In Luke 24:32, the followers of Jesus said:

Did not our heart burn within us,
while he talked with us by the way,
and while he opened to us the scriptures?

He Who Reveals Secrets

In 1973, my son Chuckie became very ill. I took him to a specialist who could not find any reason for the illness, although many tests were performed. Finally I asked the doctor if it could be leukemia. Then I told him of a dream I had about my son. When Chuckie had been four years old, I had a vision in a dream that he had leukemia. This dream was so powerful that Ken had to awaken me from it by shaking me.

The doctor ran further tests and then called me on the telephone and said, "You can rest assured, it's not leukemia." I was so relieved to hear this from the doctor, but it was a short-lived reprieve. Once more, God had prepared me for things to come.

Chuckie was later diagnosed with leukemia.

And He who reveals secrets
has made known to you what will be.
(Daniel 2:29b, NKJV)

Our Guide

After Ken and I had married, I introduced him to a former friend, Gene, who was a carpet installer. The two of them became good friends, and Ken convinced Gene to go into the carpet business with him. They were both very good at their work and their partnership was successful. Gene joined the union and Ken was non-union, allowing them to work in both areas of the market.

When Chuckie first became ill, I begged Ken to join the union to protect himself financially if the illness proved to be serious. Ken had health insurance on all of us, but I was deeply concerned that it would not protect Ken and his business. I kept trying to get Ken to go union and he kept resisting.

The doctors ran tests on Chuckie for two months and found nothing. Finally, I was to see a specialist at 10:00 on a Monday morning. Before Ken left that morning, again I asked him to go union. He said no. Then I called him at work and tried once more, "Ken please . . . I am so afraid for you."

He said, "For the last time, Arlene, NO!" and hung up on me.

I knew I had gone as far as I could with him and I began to pray, "Jesus, please take care of this situation."

At 9:00 a.m., the phone rang. It was Ken and he sounded mad, but he said, "Arlene, I just went union!"

I breathed a sigh of relief and replied, "Thanks, Ken." Then I thanked God and went to the specialist with my mother at my side. My mother went into the doctor's office with me where we heard the doctor say, "Mrs. Grant, we are going to have to send Chuckie over to the Medical Center for a bone-marrow test. This situation could be very serious, so I'm going to sign him up for Crippled Children financial assistance."

I told the doctor that wasn't necessary as we had ample insurance. But the doctor said, "No, Mrs. Grant, if the situation is what I think it is, no insurance alone is enough. If we sign him up before we find out what is wrong, he will be covered. But if we find out first, they will not cover him. Stay right here while I go and take care of the insurance papers."

We went to the hospital where Chuckie had to undergo many tests. The doctor finally came to me and told me it was leukemia. I went in to see Chuckie and he looked at me with large, pain-filled eyes and said, "Mama, do they know what's wrong?" I said "Yes" and he whispered, "Thank God, thank God." That was all he said. My son never did ask me what was wrong and I never told him.

God's hand was always upon us, guiding us and directing us through this trying time. We were to find out shortly thereafter that if Ken had not gone union when he did, we would not have had any insurance coverage for Chuckie. The agent of Ken's original policy told us that we had to have had the insurance longer for this kind of coverage and Chuckie's illness could not be covered.

The following year was filled with many things, but financial burdens were not one of them. The combined insurance policies paid for everything and Chuckie had the best of care . . . all because of a mighty God.

For this God is our God for ever and for ever:
he will be our guide even unto death.
(Psalm 48:14)

They Cannot See The Light

When Chuckie was in the hospital, many people from our church came to see him. He had reached a point where he hardly moved as he watched those around him. One day a woman came up and stood by his bed and Chuckie raised himself up on his little arms to say, "Where do you think you came from?" Then he laid back down.

The woman said, "Well, honey, I got on the elevator and came up here."

Chuckie raised himself up on his arms again, his eyes filled with distress, and said, "No. Dad, where do *you* think you came from?"

Ken was standing at the foot of the bed talking with a pastor at that moment and evidently Chuckie had been trying to resolve their conversation in his mind. Ken looked at him, smiled and returned to his conversation. Chuckie, who had asked the pastor to speak with Ken, was trying to pull his dad into heaven.

The god of this age has blinded
the minds of unbelievers, so that they cannot
see
the light of the gospel of the glory of Christ,
who is the image of God.
(2 Corinthians 4:4, NIV)

He Has Borne Our Griefs

In 1973, the elder of the church came over to pray and anoint Chuckie upstairs in his room. I went downstairs into the first bedroom to pray, to cry and to beg God for Chuckie's life. All of a sudden, I had a vision and I saw a lady in long attire with a shawl over her head. She was standing against a white stone wall crying. I said, "Mary, is that you?"

The vision immediately went to Jesus on the Cross. Mary was crying for her Son as I was crying for my son. She knew my pain and I felt that I knew hers, too. I cried for Jesus and the pain He was in and I cried for Chuckie and his pain.

Later in life I saw a television program showing the tomb where Jesus was supposed to have been buried. It was the exact place where Mary had been standing in my vision.

Surely he hath borne our griefs, and carried
our sorrows:
yet we did esteem him stricken,
smitten of God, and afflicted.
(Isaiah 53:4)

Test The Spirits

As Chuckie's condition deteriorated, I became desperate enough to try almost anything to save my child. At one point, Ken, my mother and I, took Chuckie to some natural healers who insisted that all he needed was to drink lots of juice from grass. I was ready to try even the strangest of remedies if they might help Chuckie.

Fortunately, God intervened once more and kept us out of the grasp of a very evil group that preys upon sick and hurting people who are desperate enough to grasp at straws.

Beloved, do not believe every spirit,
but test the spirits, whether they are of God;
because many false prophets have gone out
into this world.
(1 John 4:1, NKJV)

Spared From Evil

Chuckie's grandparents and I took him to see Kathryn Kuhlman. We were the first ones in line and many others were turned away because the meeting was packed. After the service started, Kathryn said there was a healing taking place in our seating area. I did not understand and took Chuckie to stand in the healing line. As we stood there, a woman came and asked what we wanted.

Chuckie said his whole body was burning up, but I did not know how healings were manifested. I whispered Chuckie's need to her and she said we were not to be in that line. I did not understand what she meant and she did not explain. Confused and very upset, I pulled Chuckie out of line and went home.

The doctors had said that Chuckie's leukemia would never go into remission, but Chuckie's illness went into remission for the following year. Perhaps he was totally healed during Katherine Kuhlman's meeting and the medicine the doctors insisted he needed was what took his life. I will only know when I see God face to face.

Chuckie died on September 18, 1974 at the age of 10.

I do know that God's holy Word states that sometimes the righteous are taken away from what is to come (Isaiah 57:1). As Chuckie and I were nearly inseparable, he would have been filled with great sorrow over the road I had chosen to walk.

*The good men perish; the godly die before
their time and no one seems to care or
wonder why. No one seems to realize that God
is taking them away from
evil days ahead.*
(Isaiah 57:1 , TLB)

We Know Not What We Should Pray

When Ken and I married, we lived in the same house that Chuck and I had bought. One night as Ken and I were in bed, I had a terrible experience. My body was asleep, but I was awake inside, screaming, "Ken, help me!" I could see him beside me, but I could not make a move to wake him. I finally came out of this state and all I could think to do was get as close to Ken as I could. I was drenched with fear, but as long as I laid very close to Ken, I felt protected.

Later, we moved to another house and I continued to sleep as close to Ken as I could. The night the doctor told me that I could rest assured that Chuckie did not have leukemia, it happened again. That night, I somehow moved away from Ken as I slept. I awoke some time later with the feeling that I was paralyzed. I felt like my body was completely dead on the outside and I was trapped on the inside, wide awake, and screaming, "Ken, help me! Help me!"

I felt as if I was trying to dig my way out of a grave, but I could not move. I struggled to move my foot, my hand, any part of my body. I felt I could come out of it if I could only move something.

When I finally did come out of this state, I was convinced that the next time it happened, I would either be possessed or I would die. I was very frightened.

After Chuckie died, we moved to another house. By now, I was nearly suffocating Ken at night, sleeping so close to him. He often asked me to move over, but

I refused unless he moved with me. One night Ken came in at three in the morning and had been drinking. He passed out on my side of the bed and I was very upset. I moved as far over onto his side as I could.

That same terrible feeling of paralysis happened again, but it was worse than it had ever been. I knew I was in dire danger. This time I didn't even think of Ken, but I screamed inside my mind, "Jesus, help me!" Instantly I saw myself in a vision. I was on my knees praying, my hands folded beneath my chin, as I repeated the words, "Orereta, Orereta, Orereta," over and over. Gradually I realized I was free to move.

I got up and wrote the strange word on a business card and put it on Kimberly's baby picture. I looked at it for a moment, having no idea what it could mean. But I did know that I was free from my previous experiences and the fear they had brought me.

We moved two more times and then I began to attend an Assemblies of God church. Curious about some of the things I saw in this church, I called my Aunt Jerry in Oklahoma and, as always, she answered the phone, "Praise the Lord."

"Aunt Jerry," I said, "have you ever spoken in an unknown tongue?"

"No, honey. Well . . . yes. I have said three words. I think they mean 'Praise the Lord.'"

The minute she spoke those words, the words "Orereta—Hallelujah," flashed across my mind. "Oh, Aunt Jerry, I have to find my word. I'll call you back."

Even though we had moved two times and several years had past, I was able to find the card with my "strange" word in just two minutes and I knew what it meant—it meant Hallelujah! In the vision I had been praising a mighty God for setting me free.

I had originally called to man for help and I was not freed. But God had wanted me to call on Him and when I did, my freedom came.

> *Likewise the Spirit also helpeth our*
> *infirmities:*
> *for we know not what we should pray for as*
> *we ought:*
> *but the Spirit itself maketh intercession for us*
> *with groanings which cannot be uttered.*
> **(Romans 8:26)**

Test Me In This

Late in 1974, Ken came to me and said, "Arlene, should we file bankruptcy?" Startled, I asked him what he meant. "We only have $1,000.00 left to run the carpet store, and we don't have any money to buy even one roll of carpet." While I had been in the hospital with Chuckie, a contractor had cheated Gene and Ken out of the money for the work they had done.

"Well, Ken, my Bible tells me that we should tithe."

"What's that?"

"We should give God ten percent of our money."

Ken looked at me in exasperation as he said, "Arlene, don't you understand? We don't have any money. God doesn't want our money."

"Ken, the widow had just two mites, that's two cents (Luke 21:2)." He just looked at me. Then I said, "I always gave my money to God, but when I married you, the money was not mine to give."

"How long do I have to give this money?"

"Whatever you tell God, Ken . . . one month, one year, whatever. But when you make a vow, you must abide by it."

He said, "Okay, I'll try it for six months."

I was thrilled and said, "Let's pray and tell God our desires." Ken said okay and together we prayed and then thanked God for what He was going to do.

A short while later, after I had begun to place our tithe in the offerings, the treasurer of my church called me. He asked, "Arlene, does your husband know you are giving this money?"

I laughed and replied, "Yes, Don, he signed the check."

He was quiet for a brief moment (I'm sure it was to look at the check) and then said, "Arlene, I'm sorry for this call."

That was in January of 1975, the beginning of a very bad year for businesses as the entire country was going through a recession. But Ken's business began to soar upward.

Ken was saved in April of 1975. Later that year, we stood in church and testified about this story. Ken said, "If I ever don't give to God, I don't know what will happen to us."

> *Bring the whole tithe into the storehouse,*
> *that there may be food in my house.*
> *Test me in this, says the Lord Almighty,*
> *and see if I will not throw open the floodgates*
> *of heaven*
> *and pour out so much blessing*
> *that you will not have room enough for it.*
> **(Malachi 3:10, NIV)**

Giving Thanks Always

In the early part of 1975, I wrote to Billy Graham and told him about the deaths of my first husband and my son. I said that I wanted prayer for the salvation of my husband, Ken. Soon thereafter a package from Billy Graham came in the mail. Inside was a pamphlet entitled, "When A Child Dies." Another pamphlet was entitled, "How a Wife Can Win Her Husband to Christ." There was other literature and a wonderful letter which commented on everything I had initially written about.

The literature arrived in the middle of the week, but I did not read it right away. I finally was able to get to it when I opened up the carpet store early the following Saturday. Alone that morning, I carefully read everything in the package. That very night, at home, I was surprised to find that Billy Graham was on television. Ken has always loved Billy Graham and that night he sat there, engrossed in the message.

After the program was over, Ken came up to me and said, "By the way . . . did you learn anything from that package Billy Graham sent on how you could win me to Christ?" I had no idea that Ken had known anything about the package I had received.

I didn't know what to say, so I offered a quick prayer, "Jesus, help me." Then I said, "No, Ken, I have done everything that little book says. I will never be a tool to help win you to God." He walked away laughing and nothing more was said.

The following Saturday night, Ken came in very late and slept in our small bedroom. He had been almost despondent all that week. The next morning I arose before anyone else and laid out everyone's church clothes. Then I took a cup of coffee and went into the tiny room we used for an office and a storage area.

Looking out the window, I smiled at the carefully tended rose garden of a little lady next door. As I gazed at the beautiful garden, I felt I could almost see Jesus walking around through the roses. I began to praise Him for the roses. Then, looking at a beautiful tree in my yard, I began to praise Him for the tree. I closed my eyes and began to praise Him for the flowers, the rain, the sky, the clouds, the rainbow and the birds.

Then I said, "I want to thank you for the good things and the bad things in my life." As I said that, Chuck flashed into my mind and then Chuckie flashed. I felt a stab in my heart as I thought to myself, "Wait a minute! What are you saying?" But I quickly spoke out, "I do, Lord, I want to thank you for the good things *and* the bad things in my life."

From the very bottom of my stomach came a violent gush of wind that went out the top of my head. I had not known it, but I had been holding Chuck's death and Chuckie's death against God. In that one moment, I was set free. In just one moment with the Master, I knew I was now able to talk about my son and share God with others.

For several months after Chuckie's death, every time I went to church, after being there for only minutes I would begin to cry. I seemed to be crying off and on all the time. After this manifestation of God's presence, I knew I could live again. I had my joy back!

*Giving thanks always for all things unto God
and the Father in the name of our Lord Jesus
Christ.*
(Ephesians 5:20)

*In every thing give thanks:
for this is the will of God in Christ Jesus
concerning you.*
(1 Thessalonians 5:18)

All Things

That same morning, when we were ready for Sunday School, Kimberly and I went into Ken's bedroom and I said, "Honey, your clothes are laid out. We're going to church now."

Ken raised himself from sleep and mumbled, "Which clothes?"

I was surprised to hear his voice and I replied, "Why, your beige outfit."

"But I wore that last time," he complained.

Kimberly, almost six, laughed as she said, "Daddy, it's been so long, those people will never remember what you wore."

I proceeded to get the children ready and, as usual, the children and I left for Sunday School and church. It was Palm Sunday. We had just sat down after the music and worship when the pastor came forward to preach. I felt a tap on my shoulder and looked up to see Ken. I moved over quickly and he slipped into the seat beside me.

The same pastor Chuckie had asked to tell his father about Jesus then proceeded to give a wonderful, Spirit-filled salvation message. That morning Ken finally walked down the aisle to surrender his life to Jesus.

I had never dreamed that Ken would give his life to God that day. All I could think about was how grateful I was to God and how I would always remember from that time forward to thank God for the good things and the bad things—all things. Ken and Kimberly were both baptized two weeks later.

*And we know that all things work together
for good to them that love God,
to them who are the called according to his
purpose.*
(Romans 8:28).

All These Things Shall Be Added

In 1973 and 1976 I had gone out periodically looking for land to build our home. My children and I had looked at a lot of land and somehow I always ended up in Elk Grove. One day I finally found a place where there were only four or five new homes and lots of land. I was excited! I inquired about the land and was told that it alone was not for sale. It could only be sold with a home already built on it. I told them I had cash to pay for it, and then gave them my name and number and asked them to please call me if they ever changed their minds.

When I told Ken, he said, "Arlene, they will never sell you that land. The contractor I've been doing carpet for has a piece of land we could buy right now and it's down the street from where you want to build." He took me over to see it, and I sat in the truck because I knew where I wanted to build.

I continued to pray for the piece of property that they said I could not have. "Please, God, work us a miracle." One day we went over to the property that the contractor had told Ken he would sell to us.

Ken got out and walked off the land while I sat in the truck. He came back and got in the truck and said, "Okay, if you want to have a home, it's up to you! I've had it." He gunned the gas and sped off. He did not talk to me again about building me a home. I kept praying and hoping for the land that we "could not have."

Two months went by and one day the phone rang. It was the people who owned the land that I wanted.

They had decided to sell parcels to outside contractors who had cash for the land and plans that they could approve for their subdivision. I was so excited! Ken could not believe the good news.

We took Kim and Ken, Jr. (I was pregnant again) and drove out to the land. As we held hands in a circle and prayed, we thanked God for giving us our heart's desire and allowing us to see His awesome power. God changes hearts and situations.

> *But seek ye first the kingdom of God, and his righteousness; and all these things shall be added unto you.*
> **(Matthew 6:33)**

When I Make Up My Jewels

When my children were being born, the hospital staff had me take off my jewelry and give it to my husband. But when Julie was born, I continued to wear my wedding ring. After she was born, the nurse took her away to get her dressed. I kept thanking God that the birth was over and behind me.

As I lay on the delivery table, I allowed my hand to dangle over the side. I felt something touch my hand and I looked over the edge of the table to see this tiny, wee hand reaching for my diamond ring. It was my baby, Julie, on a little cart the nurse had rolled up beside me.

Julie is still reaching up for the jewels God has prepared for each of His children. She is the one who tells others of the coming rapture that is going to take place. Julie is distinctly Julie, a present sent from God, a priceless treasure.

And they shall be mine, saith the Lord of hosts, in that day when I make up my jewels, and I will spare them as a man spareth his own son that serveth him.
(Malachi 3:17)

Get Understanding

When Julie was born, we began to call her, "Julie Elaine, pretty little thing." She loved that name as she grew older. When her sister, Tiffany, was born, we named her Tiffany Raylene, pretty little queen." Julie didn't understand and said, "I don't want to be a thing anymore."

I just looked at her and quickly said to myself, "Oh, Lord, help!"

Then she asked, "What is a thing, anyway?"

"Oh, you know, a thing is a rose, a diamond, a ruby, a queen, anything you want it to be."

"Okay, I'll be a thing." Now she had understanding and it was all right. We must have understanding. In the Book of Proverbs, we are told that above all else, get understanding. Each one of us needs understanding in every area of our lives.

Wisdom is supreme; therefore get wisdom.
Though it cost all you have, get
understanding.
(Proverbs 4:7, NIV)

May His Name Endure

Kimberly Dawn, pretty little swan. Kenneth Ray, king for a day. Julie Elaine, pretty little thing. Tiffany Raylene, pretty little queen. We made each child feel that special names were always important.

May his name endure forever;
may it continue as long as the sun.
All nations will be blessed through him,
and they will call him blessed.
(Psalm 72:17, NIV)

. . . And (I) will give him a white stone,
and in the stone a new name written . . .
(Revelation 2:17b)

Possible With God

With my daughter, Tiffany, nothing is impossible. Out of all my children, Tiffany reminds me the most of Chuckie. She has built-in wisdom and takes grownup problems and dissects them, bringing them to an understanding. She has a lot of beauty and kindness within her. She believes that God can do the impossible and her faith is tremendous.

If we pray for a parking place, Tiffany believes it will be there. When Chuckie was going to the hospital all the time, he would pray for a parking place and it would be there. There are many things that Tiffany has gone through and seen in her young life. She's a treasure, as are all of my children.

Jesus replied, "What is impossible with men
is possible with God."
(Luke 18:27, NIV)

Whom The Son Sets Free

I had been a Baptist all of my life. When someone would ask me what I was, I would say, "I'm a Baptist, but I'm a free spirit." When we moved to Elk Grove in Northern California, Sharon (Ken's sister) called me and asked what church I was attending. I replied that I was church hopping and my kids were quite upset with me. We were not getting spiritually fed anywhere, it seemed.

Sharon had been going to another little church and she said she wasn't getting fed, either. Then she said, "I have heard that there is a little church in Florin where people are really getting the Word."

I got very excited because Florin was only a few miles from me, but the prospect of getting fed was even more important. Sharon knew I was a Baptist, so when I asked her what denomination this little church was, she hesitantly replied, "It's Assemblies of God."

I immediately said, "Oh, Sharon, those people hang from chandeliers."

Sharon laughed and said, "Look, you pray about it. I'll pray about it. Call me on Saturday."

We both prayed and when we talked on Saturday, I felt compelled to go. Little did I know that this would be what God had ordained for the next three years of my life. I was sorry when the pastor of this congregation moved to another church after those three years. I felt that the strong biblical Word he brought forth was only his particular preaching and if I had to break in another new preacher, I might as well do it closer to my house. So I began to attend the Assemblies of God church only two blocks from where I lived. I found that most Assemblies' preachers bring the Word of God in truth.

God wants us to be free spirits—free in mind, body and soul.

> *If the Son therefore shall make you free,*
> *ye shall be free indeed.*
> **(John 8:36)**

Sheep's Clothing

Ken's sister, Sharon, asked me to go to a weekend seminar revival meeting with her and two other girlfriends. We would get one room with two beds, she told me.

I talked it over with Ken, as I had never been anywhere without my family. I was able to go and when we left on Friday night, everything seemed magical. I could feel God's Spirit. I could feel the power of God all around me. I was so completely overwhelmed, I could have taken my one-karat diamond wedding ring off and put it into the offering plate.

I was very excited all day Saturday, but by that evening, I felt heavy. Something just wasn't right with the speaker's ministry—but I didn't know what it was. By the time we were finally ready to leave, I wanted to run away from the place.

We were all walking through the hallway to get outside and the girls were still very excited. They asked me, "What did you think?" They should have known better than to ask me that question.

"Well, I'll tell you what I think." I said. "Lord," I prayed, "help me show them." I randomly opened the pages of my Bible to the one Scripture about wolves in sheep's clothing. That was exactly what was wrong, I realized.

God was always my shield and now He was my guide. The Scriptures say to try the spirits. That is what my spirit was doing and it found the speaker's spirit to be wrong. Today, there is a problem in this man's ministry. There always was, I believe. The Word of God tells us that every secret thing will come to light. Thank you, Father.

For God will bring every deed into judgment
including every hidden thing whether it is
good or evil.
(Ecclesiastes 12:14, NIV)

The Truth Will Set You Free

Several months later, a couple we had periodically spoken to on the phone (they had been married on the base the same day as Ken and I) accepted Ken's invitation to come to California to visit. They drove from Chicago, Illinois, to spend their vacation with us.

We were awaiting their arrival and finally heard their knock on the door. Ken went to the door and after a brief conversation, the door closed and Ken came back to where I was waiting. "Arlene, they say they are not going to stay."

"But, why not?" I asked.

"Well, when I opened the door to them, they saw the picture of Jesus and said they could not stay with us. When I asked why, they said, 'We are big leaders in the Jehovah's Witness movement.' They planned to attend some meetings while here in California."

"Ken, you go tell them if they can lay their religion down for one week, I certainly can lay my religion down for a week. We won't even talk of religious things. We will just be friends, one on one." Ken went back out and the couple agreed they could stay with us under those conditions.

It had seemed so logical and simple when I first proposed the idea, but the decision wasn't easy to live with. I prayed and prayed and prayed, telling the Lord how hard it was to keep my word. "Lord, I will not say one word unless You put the words in my mouth. I know they must come from You."

Every morning, Ken and I and this couple sat in the living room in exactly the same places and every morning they brought up something about the "movement." I said nothing, but, oh, how I would pray in my spirit.

The last day of their visit, as we sat in the living room in the exact same places, they produced a big stack of books for Ken. They were clearly not keeping their part of the bargain, but still I said nothing and continued to pray. "Lord, I have said nothing—what do You want me to do? Lord, show me."

Suddenly the words began to come forth and I spoke directly to the husband. "Tell me something. Now this is hypothetical, but imagine you are now on your way home with your family. Tell me, what would you do if you had an accident and your whole family was killed?"

He looked at me and replied, "Well, I would pray!"

"Who would you pray to?"

He paused and then answered, "The Holy Spirit."

His wife jumped up and said, "We don't even believe in the Holy Spirit!"

I knew from that revelation in this man's spirit that God had been answering my prayers. His soul had begun to think towards the truth. The Word of God says that when we know the truth, the truth shall set us free.

Then you will know the truth,
and the truth will set you free.
(John 8:32, NIV)

You And Your Household

I was not allowed to go out until I was eighteen, but I was allowed to go to all church functions. My dad even took us all to a Billy Graham crusade in Sacramento where I attended classes to be a counselor. My dad had finally decided that if there was a heaven, he would be going there because he had let his children go to church. One day he would have to face that choice.

I prayed for his salvation throughout my life. I loved my dad. He never showed us love physically, but we knew he loved us. One day my dad was way up on a back road in the hills near Colfax and he went down in the canyon to feed his cows. On the way home, he was traveling on Sunshine Valley Road, a dangerously narrow and winding road.

My dad saw a car parked alongside the road with its hood up and he stopped to see if the man was having car trouble. The man was a man of God and after they talked, he asked Dad if he knew Jesus Christ. Dad said "No." The man then asked if he would like to accept Jesus into his life and my dad said "Yes."

The man led Dad in a prayer of salvation. My dad was overjoyed. He came home calling, "Daisy, I just accepted Jesus into my heart! Call all the girls and tell them."

My dad, who had never studied the Bible, needed his mind trained in the way it should go. He learned a lot about God through his children. This was our main desire for our dad in all our lives.

Believe in the Lord Jesus, and you will be
saved you and your household.
(Acts 16:31 NIV)

Turn The Hearts Of The Fathers

Not only does the mind need training, but the heart needs healing and training, too. I reflect back on a poem that goes something like this:

There are two natures beneath my breast,
One is cursed, the other is blessed.
The one I love, the one I hate,
The one I feed will dominate
(Author unknown).

As the day drew near when Ken and I and the kids were to leave on vacation in 1980, I suddenly felt I had to call my dad. I went to the phone and dialed his number, anxious to hear his voice. When he answered, I said, "Dad, I'm really worried about you."

He said, like so many times before, "About what?"

"About whether or not you know Jesus."

"Well, Arlene, what makes you think I don't?"

"That's all I wanted to know, Dad."

Just before we left, Dad and Mom came to our house for dinner. As we walked out to the car to leave, Dad put his arms around me and said, "My baby, my baby!" That was the only compassion I ever received from him. Hugging that moment inside of my heart, we left for Kansas.

I will send you the prophet Elijah before that great
and dreadful day of the Lord comes. He will turn the
hearts of the fathers to their children, and the hearts
of the children to their fathers.
(Malachi 4:5-6, NIV)

I Cry Aloud

After we arrived in Kansas, the children and I were going to stay with Ken's aunt and uncle for a few days while Ken went on with a friend to the car races. Shortly after Ken left, I received a phone call that my dad had been killed.

I was devastated and in a state of shock. My husband was not with me and my dad had been killed. I cried out to God, "God, help me! Help me!" When I called, Ken had not yet arrived at his destination. I left a message for him to call me and went to bed crying for my dad. "What about Ken, Lord?" I prayed. "Is he all right?" I lay there in the dark, in pain, and full of questions. I began to see a white van going in and out of shadows. Then I somehow had a glimpse of the inside of the van, and saw someone lying down in the back. Instantly I knew Ken was all right. He was still in transit and had not arrived at his destination.

I was able to forget about my concerns for Ken and focus on my children and praying for my family's strength. Ken called me the next day and advised me on what to do and how to get home quickly to my mother, brother and sisters. Then Ken told me he had slept in the back of the van as Ralph drove through the night.

To the Lord I cry aloud, and he answers me from his holy hill. I lie down and sleep; I wake again, because the Lord sustains me.
(Psalm 3:4-5, NIV)

Weapons Of Our Warfare

In 1982, we went to Chicago to visit the couple who were Jehovah's Witnesses. When we arrived, they showed us our room and I began to feel very heavy in my spirit. I prayed, "Lord, help these people find you."

As I was praying, my daughter came into the room crying. She asked me a question about Jesus. I knew that the battle was raging as the enemy was trying to confuse and upset us with wrong doctrine. I put my arms about my daughter and began to pray with her. Then I said, "Jesus, help us find a Scripture to help Kim." I opened up my Bible and there was exactly the word that she needed to hear. Kim walked away victorious.

No sooner was that battle won than Ken came into the room. "Arlene, I've got to find something in the Bible," and he proceeded to ask me where a certain Scripture was.

"I'm not sure," I said, "but let's pray." After we had prayed, I opened the Bible to the exact verse Ken needed. He grabbed the Bible from me and ran back to defend our Lord and His truth. I continued to pray until I finally got the assurance that God was in control. As long as we were standing on His Word, I knew everything would be okay. I felt His peace for the first time in that house.

The next day, we all went out to get Mexican food. The hot sauce was bubbling in a funny sort of way, almost like a mini volcano. "Ken," I cautioned, "I wouldn't eat that sauce. I think it's spoiled."

Ken told our friends what I had said, then they questioned the waitress. She quickly tried to reassure us, "Oh, no, it's always like that."

"Well, my children must not eat the hot sauce!" I announced. And my kids did not eat it. Ken laughed, and everyone ate the sauce anyway.

All night long and into the next day, everyone who had eaten the hot sauce was fighting over the bathrooms. They all had food poisoning and were deathly ill. The kids were crying in pain.

We finished our visit without any more attacks.

For the weapons of our warfare are not
carnal, but mighty through God
to the pulling down of strong holds.
(2 Corinthians 10:4)

Hope As An Anchor

There was hurt and frustration at every turn of my marriage. I clung to God who was the only anchor in my life. Prayer was what helped me to stay sane.

I never could put my finger on what the problem was, except Ken was not walking with God.

We have this hope as an anchor for the soul,
firm and secure.
(Hebrews 6:19, NIV)

In A Dream

Ken became good friends with a man he met at the races. One Saturday the man suggested that they buy a good sprint car together and he would take it to Australia and race it. Ken was excited about the deal.

That night, as I went to bed, I was troubled about this venture and I began to pray earnestly. The next afternoon Ken called and said, "Arlene, bring the money over here. We want to buy this car." His friend did not have his share of the money, but he told Ken that he was expecting it the following week.

"Please, Ken, we can't buy anything on Sunday—it's the Lord's day. Let's buy it tomorrow," I pleaded. Ken got very upset and hung up the phone. I didn't know what to do except continue to pray.

When he came home later that night, he said, "Well, the man was very upset. They'll probably sell that car before we can buy it." I assured him that if it was God's will, the car would still be there when it was time to buy it.

When I fell asleep that night, I dreamed that Ken's friend came over with a lady friend and Ken wanted to take us all out to dinner. The man said, "I haven't had time to clean my suit. It's in the car, but the pants are too soiled to wear."

"Not to worry," I assured him, "bring the pants in. I will launder them, and we can go have a good time."

He brought the pants to me and I put them in my machine on the gentle cycle with Woolite. I was very careful with them, but when I took them out of the washer, the whole pocket was eaten away. There was nothing but a big hole where the pocket had been. In the dream, I was mortified and didn't know what to do.

The next day I went to my husband and pleaded with him to listen, "Please, Ken, let's wait for this man's money. I don't believe he has any."

"Arlene, he does!" Ken replied. Then I told him about my dream. After he had thought about it for awhile, he decided to wait. The man never came back to the races. And, praise the Lord, Ken never bought a race car.

> *In a dream, in a vision of the night, when deep sleep falleth upon men, in slumberings upon the bed; then he openeth the ears of men, and sealeth their instruction.*
> **(Job 33:15-16)**

Lovers Of Their Own Selves

We spent thousands on sprint car races. These races were slowly consuming our lives, taking up our family time, our vacation time and all spare time. I was slowly dying inside. Ken and I were no longer friends. I was nothing but a warm body to him. I longed for a different relationship with Ken. In 1984, near the breaking point, I sat down and began to write out my feelings. I wrote in such big letters that the hurtful words took up nine pages:

I hate to sit in cars
I hate racing because
I always stay in the car
I don't like to sit in the car!

I hate racing because
you have always
acted like you are single.
You have always done your thing.

I no longer want to go
anywhere with you anymore
because you love yourself
and only yourself!

The kids don't even exist
when it comes to you.
They're last,
just like me!

"HATE"

I was hurting and my kids were hurting. Jesus was all that kept me sane. I didn't know what to do. I had blown it bad, but I was married and I loved Ken. I kept saying over and over, "What do I do now? Jesus, please help me."

And that which fell among thorns are they, which, when they have heard, go forth, and are choked with cares and riches and pleasures of this life, and bring no fruit to perfection.
(Luke 8:14)

For men shall be lovers of their own selves.
(2 Timothy 3:2a)

Trust In The Lord

One day when Ken Jr. was twelve years old, he was upstairs waiting for his grandmother. The kids were going to her house for the weekend and Ken and I were going to the lake. Ken Jr. had the window open and his ghetto blaster was playing. Suddenly, a twenty-year-old man ran out of his house and into the neighbor's yard where he shot at Ken Jr. with a high-powered pellet gun. The pellet broke the window and just missed my son. We called the police and made out a report, but nothing ever came of it.

From that day on, our lives changed. Ken Jr., a loving and obedient son, had been making good grades in school. But when this happened, the tables turned. He began breaking things, yelling, screaming and refusing to sleep in his room. I had received a letter from the Victim Witness program telling me that he could get counseling if he needed it—if we responded within one year. I put the letter on the shelf, determined that God and I would take care of the circumstance.

One month before the year was up, I was walking the floor one night to stay awake. I was frightful that my son would come in and kill the whole family. I was in much prayer. Finally I called and made an appointment to get counseling for Ken Jr.

The counselor said that it was like Ken Jr. had been on a plane that had crashed, but he did not get killed. Ken Jr. was in a very devastating trauma situation that he could not handle. The counseling continued and my prayers continued.

After a year, the counselor said, "He is now back in his room. I feel that the counseling should stop."

"Oh, no. No! I have a great fear of him doing something to my family," I said.

"Well, I can run some extensive testing. It will cost a great deal, but the State will pay for half of it." I agreed and Ken Jr. was tested. When the time came to receive the results of the tests, I went by the store to get my husband Ken. "Honey, the results of Ken's tests will be ready tonight," I said. "Are you going with me?"

Ken replied, "No, you go and find out what he says. Then you tell me." I went alone.

The counselor said, "Mrs. Grant, Ken's slipping in reading." I knew Ken Jr. had not wanted to do anything since the shooting. The counselor continued, "Ken has three times more common sense than other children his age." I thought about how important common sense was and how all our family had a lot of common sense.

Then the counselor dropped the bomb! "What is wrong with this boy is he comes from an alcoholic parent!"

"Now, you wait just a minute," I cried out. "My husband may be a heavy drinker, but he is not an alcoholic!"

"Mrs. Grant, my advice is that you don't walk to the nearest Al-Anon, you run!"

I felt myself going into shock. I went back to the store and they told me Ken was in the back. I said, "I'm going next door to have tea." I wanted to sort things out and pray. I finally went back to the store and learned that Ken had left and gone home. And, yes, they told me, he was drunk.

For another year, I continued to put Al-Anon on a shelf. God and I could take care of this. I prayed and stood still. Everything got worse.

Trust in the Lord with all your heart
and lean not on your own understanding:
in all your ways acknowledge him,
and he will make your paths straight.
(Proverbs 3:5-6, NIV)

Rejoice

Our carpet store was doing very well and Ken had the carpet, wallpaper, lino and drapes contract for several housing tracts. On one contract, Ken had bid the job low, based on a very good price he was able to get on carpet from Georgia. The only catch was that this carpet would take longer than usual to get. The contractor agreed that this wasn't a problem.

However, the late shipment was a problem. It did not arrive when expected and the contractor threatened to cancel our contract. Every morning I called Georgia at 5:00 a.m. (to allow for a three-hour time difference from the West Coast) and even before, hoping that someone would answer. Every conversation always ended in, "It's on the way!" Unfortunately, "on the way" wasn't going to cut it with the contractor.

I prayed and prayed. Getting out my Bible, I prayed for a word. When I turned to Philippians 4:6 in my Living Bible, I read, *"Don't worry about anything and instead pray about everything. Tell God your needs and don't forget to thank Him for His answers."* This wonderful Scripture instantly took me out of my turmoil, hurt and depression.

When Ken came home that night, he looked haggard, as if he had aged years overnight. I looked at him and said, "Lord, let me feel what he's feeling. Let me back in it with him."

But the Lord said, *"No, my daughter. You have been released. Be full of joy in the Lord. I say it again, rejoice!"*

The carpet finally came and was installed, but the contractor said he didn't have the money to pay Ken.

Ken went through a great deal more stress and trouble before he was able to get his money. After this period of stress, Ken decided to sell the business.

> *Rejoice in the Lord always:*
> *and again I say, Rejoice.*
> **(Philippians 4:4)**

I Will . . . Show Thee Great And Mighty Things

One day Ken came to me, very discouraged, after a prospective buyer for our carpet store had cancelled his appointment with us.

I looked deep into his eyes and asked, "You really do want to sell the business?"

"More than you'll ever know, Arlene."

I said, "Ken, let's pray!" He agreed and we knelt at the foot of the bed and prayed.

When we stood up, Ken said, "Well?"

I looked at him and laughed. He wanted God to say something to me right then. I went into the kitchen, still laughing about his expectations. I began to make tea and when I dipped the tea bag into the hot water, it was as if I knew why the man had cancelled his appointment with us. I went back to the bedroom and said, "Ken, I think I know why he is not buying Colony House." Boy, did that get Ken's attention!

"Why?" he responded quickly.

"Because he doesn't have the money."

"Arlene, don't you understand? He does have the money."

"Yes, Ken he does—but it's all tied up." Then I walked back into the living room.

In about ten minutes Ken came in and asked, "Do you really believe his money is tied up?" I told him yes. "Then, Arlene, if you believe that—call him!" I calmly said that I would. "You really do believe his money is tied up?" Ken urged me to respond again. When I reassured him that I did believe that, he said, "Then I'll call him."

Ken called the man and explained that he thought we could work something out for the sale and asked him and his wife to keep their appointment with us. They agreed. At 2:00 p.m. that day, Ken and I and the wife were seated. The man was still standing, looking at Ken. Finally he said, "I have to level with you. I have the money to buy Colony House, but it's all tied up."

Ken looked at me, smiled, and said, "That's what I thought. I think we can work this out!" Wow! All because of a great and mighty God.

Call unto me, and I will answer thee, and shew thee great and mighty things, which thou knowest not.
(Jeremiah 33:3)

My God Shall Supply

We sold our carpet store and purchased a small mini-mart. Somehow, everything seemed to go crazy with the economy at once and we were about to go under financially. We needed money badly. I began to pray through my tears.

I had not dreamed of my dad since he died in 1980, but this night he came to me in a dream and said, "Baby, ask Mama for the money."

I said, "Daddy, Mama doesn't have it."

He said again, "Just ask Mama for the money."

The next morning, I was up very early and I called her, although I had no idea what she would say. "Mama, I don't know why I'm calling you, but Daddy came to me last night in a dream and I told him I needed money. He said to go to you. So, here I am!"

My mama calmly replied, "How much do you need?"

Surprised, I asked, "Well, how much could you lend us?"

"I have a $20,000.00 T-bill that's up this week."

"Mama, if I pay you the same interest, could I borrow it?"

"Yes, you can." I had never borrowed money from my mama before. But when my dad rescued me through a dream by sending me to her, the money was ready right on time.

But my God shall supply all your need according to his riches in glory by Christ Jesus.
(Philippians 4:19)

Come Out From Among Them

In February of 1985, God put the skids on racing for me and my family.

Julie came to me and said, "Mama, I dreamed a bad dream last night . . . about you and Daddy. Daddy was driving really fast. The sun was in both your eyes and neither of you could do anything to prevent a bad car accident. You drove into the ocean. We were left alone and Kimberly had to take care of me and Tiffany. Mama, I didn't have a mama or daddy anymore. I was so sad."

I wrote down all the words of Julie's dream on a piece of paper. Then I wrote the letters N.M.R.P.J. just in case Ken ran across it. They stood for "*No More Racing, Please Jesus.*"

God was even in my sorrow, being my friend every minute, always there for me to talk to. He was bringing us slowly out of the bondage we had created. After this dream, we no longer spent every weekend in sorrow. Ken went to the races by himself from that day forward.

Wherefore come out from among them,
and be ye separate, saith the Lord.
(2 Corinthians 6:17a)

Mourning Into Dancing

It was early in the morning, the twelfth anniversary of the loss of my first son, Charles. This had always been a hard day for me. And now I was in a battle for Ken's soul and my marriage. I began to fast and pray and cry for my joy. I searched in the Word. I continued to fast and pray all day, for my family was in sackcloth. I knew that Jesus had said to His disciples:

"If ye have faith as a grain of mustard seed, ye shall say unto this mountain, Remove hence to yonder place; and it shall remove; and nothing shall be impossible unto you. Howbeit this kind goeth not out but by prayer and fasting"
(Matthew. 17:20-21).

Thursday, Friday and Saturday, I was fasting, praising, singing, crying for our joy. Nothing happened. When I woke up Sunday morning, I finally washed my face and ate a bowl of cereal. I said, "Jesus, three days and three nights. Please save his soul. I want nothing else for this man."

In church that morning, the pastor preached on trials, hurts and problem situations. He called for raised hands of those who were going through trials. I didn't raise my hand, but I knew I was going to go forward to the altar. The pastor paused and then said, "There is someone else." His words penetrated my spirit and I shot up both hands.

I stood to my feet and moved toward the front of the church. Then I heard the words, *"Go, get your son and daughter."*

"Oh, Lord, Kenny will be embarrassed."

"I will take care of Kenny."

I turned to where Kenny was standing and said, "Son, go up there with Mama."

"Oh, Mom, come on." Kenny said.

"Son, I need you!"

Kenny didn't hold back another second and walked behind me. We started toward my daughter, Kimberly, and she had already begun walking towards us with tears streaming down her face. We reached the front and knelt at the center of the altar, the three of us, to pray and receive.

A few seconds passed and I heard a voice speak out behind us with a word of knowledge: "Here we are, Lord—Shadrach, Meshach and Abednego, in the fiery, burning furnace. But there You are, Lord, walking in their midst."

These words brought our joy back, completely releasing our hurt, fear and anger. When I had raised both hands in response to the tug of the Spirit, they were tools, one for me and one for my son. My daughter had already raised her own hand.

The three of us were walking in the burning furnace and if we had not obeyed, we would not have received the joy the Lord wanted for the three of us, His children:

> *Fasting, Obeying and Praising*
> *Shadrach, Meshach and Abednego.*
> **(Daniel 3:26,27)**

That evening I went up to the man who had given the word of knowledge and thanked him for obeying God. I told him that his obedience had completely brought our joy back. He replied, "You know, it was so funny. I saw you going up and then I heard, *'Go tell her about Shadrach, Meshach and Abednego.'* I replied, 'But, Lord, there is only one of her.' I heard again, *'Go tell her about Shadrach, Meshach and Abednego.'* By the time I got to the front, there were three of you."

Thou has turned for me my mourning into dancing;
thou has put off my sackcloth, and girded me with gladness.
(Psalm 30:11)

Do You Love Me?

Later that afternoon, I was lost in prayer, talking and praising, singing and dancing, with my Lord. I heard myself say, "Lord! I think I know what is wrong with my marriage, besides the drinking." I felt His Spirit was very close. I knew He was listening very carefully.

"Lord, when I first married Ken, he thought an older woman was a feather in his cap. Then as I got older, the younger women were in abundance. So, Lord, to Ken, I must seem old."

I was shocked to hear the Lord say with great warmth, *"Arlene?"*

As a little girl, I had learned all about Samuel and how God had talked to him. So, when I heard my name, I knew it was God and I responded quickly, "Yes, Lord?"

"Do you love Me?"

"Oh, Lord, I love You more than life itself. You are Alpha and Omega, the Beginning and the End. You are my God."

"Arlene?"

"Yes, Lord?"

"How old am I?"

"Ah, well . . . I know you are more than 2,000 years old."

"Do you still love Me?"

Warmth and contentment entered my heart. If I loved Jesus more than life itself, and He was over 2,000

years old, then love truly had nothing to do with "age."
"Thank You, Lord, for always being exactly what I
need. The devil lost again!"

> *He saith to him again the second time,*
> *Simon, son of Jonas, lovest thou me?*
> *He saith unto him, Yea, Lord; thou knowest*
> *that I love thee.*
> *He saith unto him,* **Feed my sheep.**
> **(John 21:16)**

Trust in the Lord

I finally started going to Al-Anon, but in name only. I chose to run away from what was facing me at home. Everyone at Al-Anon knew me as Sophia. My name is Sophia Arlene.

Sophia means wisdom, but I am not wise. Arlene means pledge and that suited me, for I had truly pledged my life to God when I was seven years old.

I learned a lot in Al-Anon.

Trust in the Lord with all thine heart;
and lean not unto thine own understanding.
(Proverbs 3:5)

Thy Word Is a Lamp

By 1986 my marriage was falling apart. I was desperate, crying and begging God for help. Driving down the highway late one night, I began to scream at the top of my lungs, "Please, God, what is wrong with my marriage? Help me!" I reached home and stumbled out of my car into the dark, still shaking and crying.

Once inside the house, I got my Bible, went into the front bathroom, and prayed, "God, please give me guidance. Please let me know what is wrong with my marriage." I continued to cry and pray. I opened my Bible and my eyes fell on Romans 14:21: "It is good neither to eat flesh, nor drink wine, nor anything whereby thy brother stumbleth, or is offended, or is made weak."

I stared at that Scripture. I had read it many times in my life, but this time the Scripture opened up to me. After I had Tiffany, my third daughter, I was very anemic. My son, Chuckie, was anemic when he was born and had died with leukemia, cancer of the blood. My doctor had told me to drink one or two small glasses of wine a night for my blood, so I did. I had not felt any guilt or any remorse at doing so, excusing this with the words that Jesus had drank wine. I kept looking at the Scripture and saw my small glass of wine. Then I saw Ken's large glass of wine. I had made myself his drinking partner.

I had been in complete denial, convinced that it was all Ken's problem, not mine. I knew Ken was an alcoholic, but when I was told to take the wine for my blood, I never realized that I was going directly against God.

I began to cry again as I asked God to forgive me. I told Him I would rather be anemic than transgress against His Word. Then something unusual happened. I looked at the Scripture again because I did not want to ever forget this particular verse that God had showed me.

Funny little memory "helpers," Romans 14:21, began to come into my mind. I teased Ken about having "roamin" hands when we were dating. My youngest son was fourteen and my oldest son was twenty-one.

I began to reflect on why Ken and my two sons were the "helpers" that had come to my mind. These two sons had often commented on their dad's drinking. Six months after we found out that Chuckie had leukemia, even he had asked, "Mama, is it because of me that my father drinks?"

I replied, "No, son," but I could think of no other words. Chuckie had even got Ken to sign a vow which said: *"I will never drink again. Ken."* Ken Jr. had also gotten his dad to sign a vow several years later.

Romans 14:21 had completely released me from ever wanting to take another drink of alcohol. This Scripture gave me the understanding that I needed to see that the wine had come between God and me. I asked God to forgive me and take my desire for alcohol away. I have never desired to drink alcohol of any kind since.

Thy word is a lamp unto my feet,
and a light unto my path.
(Psalm 119:105)

Prayer . . . Is Powerful

When my son, Ken Jr., was eighteen years old, he was upstairs with a friend who was spending the night at our house. In the middle of the night, I awoke and began to walk the floor, crying and praying. I kept asking God what was happening, what was going on. I began to praise God until I got some relief and was able to go back to bed and to sleep.

In the very early hours of the morning, my son and this boy knocked on our door. "Son, what are you doing outside?" I asked. "What is going on?"

"I crawled out the window upstairs, Mom. I was going to leave and never come back. We left town and started going to Chico. I was riding along and I heard, *"Now Mama doesn't have anyone."* Mom, I heard my brother's voice, Chuckie's voice, say, *"Now Mama doesn't have anyone."* So I said, 'Brian, turn this van around and take me home.' I'm sorry, Mom, and I love you."

The prayer of a righteous man
is powerful and effective.
(James 5:16b, NIV)

You Who Are Spiritual

My eldest daughter Kimberly went to Bible school at age eighteen to study biblical counseling, a dream she had long held. Frustrated with waiting on God's timing for a mate, she told Him she would find her own boyfriend. Within a year, she was dating a man who was twenty-seven. I dreamed one night that she was pregnant. I cried and cried in the dream. I went to my pastor's wife, Lois, and whispered my dream in her ear. She replied, "Oh, no!" She knew my hurts.

God was preparing me for what was coming. It wasn't even three months later when Kim came to me and confessed that she was expecting a baby. I didn't cry. I didn't accuse her. I had already worked my way through the shock and pain.

Still feeling a mother's disappointment and pain for her child, I went to the altar to ask God's direction. To my utter amazement, I heard God say, *"Barry will be the father of your grandchildren."* This was God's confirmation and Kim's cross that she would have to bear. Her choices had put her into the furnace of affliction.

If someone is caught in a sin,
you who are spiritual should restore him
gently.
(Galatians 6:1, NIV)

Your Mother's Teaching

With a fellow worker as a passenger, Ken Jr. was driving his car through town one day. He looked briefly down to change a tape and he hit the car in front of him.

The man in that car had a baby in the front seat without any seat restraints. The baby was thrown to the floor. Ken's passenger said, "Boy, Ken, your insurance is going to go up sky high!"

When the driver of the other vehicle got out to look at the damage done, he said to Ken Jr., "You can tell that this is your fault."

Ken Jr. said, "Yes, sir, and I'm sorry. Is the baby hurt?"

"No, and we can forget this whole thing if you just give me $50.00."

Ken Jr. paused as if looking out into space as the words of his earlier teachings returned to him, *"Obey the laws of the land."* So he said, "Mister, I'm going to go over to that phone booth and call the police and my insurance company right now. I'll be right back." And Ken headed for the phone booth.

The man hollered, "Later, buddy!" and took off, and Ken Jr. never saw him again. God rewarded his obedience to the truths he had been taught as a child.

My son, keep your father's commands
and do not forsake your mother's teaching.
Bind them upon your heart forever; fasten them
around your neck. When you walk, they will guide
you: when you sleep, they will watch over you: when
you awake, they will speak to you.
(Proverbs 6:20-22, NIV)

The Joy Of The Lord

In April of 1988, Ken and I were walking to the drug store to get some medication for Julie and then go out for a pizza. It was getting quite late and I prayed that we would get there on time. Ken ran on ahead of me and when he got to the door, the man inside said, "We're closed, it's nine o'clock." Ken turned and began walking back towards me. I started to run toward him.

When Ken told me that the store was closed, I said, "No, I have to have that medicine!" I went up to the door and found it was still open. I said to the man inside, "Sir, my husband was just here for some medicine."

The man said, "Well, the pharmacist is gone."

"But, the medicine has already been prepared. Please check," I implored.

Begrudgingly, he replied, "Well, okay, if the pharmacist is still there." Thankfully, I was able to get the medicine.

On the way back home, I was not aware that Ken had already been drinking. We got into several heated arguments and Ken decided we would skip the pizza. As we walked, I said, "Please, Ken, I'm as close to perfect for you as you'll ever find. Please, let's be happy! I have loved you so much for over twenty years."

He replied, "For the millionth time, I'm getting a divorce."

I wanted to get away from the accusations I knew would come and started to run. Ken sprinted past me.

I stopped running and began to walk. I was hurting, praying and crying as I turned down our very dark and secluded street. I began praising God and moved into deep praise as I walked, and for the first time in my life, I spoke in tongues. I spoke fast and abruptly, then there was a pause and once again the language of tongues flowed out of me fast and abruptly.

Then a melody of words began to pour into my mind and I heard these first words: *"Greatness will follow you."* In my spirit, I saw my grandson, who I believe represented all my grandchildren to come. I knew it was a revelation of spiritual knowledge.

At that moment God showed me that I had married Ken for a very important work. My marriage was like the back of a tapestry with all the knots and threads showing, but the front side of a tapestry is beautiful to one who can see it—just like God sees His perfect plan for our lives.

The complete word of knowledge was, *"Greatness will follow you. You have loved me more than words can say. You will not remain in this sorrow. You have been rewarded."*

I began to laugh with joy, and I laughed and laughed. Just me and the Lord, all alone in the dark, sharing joy. I barely noticed it at first for it was so dark, but a truck passed me very slowly and then it began backing up towards me. "Oh, Lord, You'll have to help me." I clutched my can of Mace tightly.

The truck stopped in front of me and I heard a familiar voice call out to me. It was my son! He said, "Mom, is that you?" I asked him how he could tell it was me in the dark. He laughed and said, "Mom, I'd know your walk anywhere!"

I laughed with him. I had my joy back and I felt strong again. The joy of the Lord is our strength!

The joy of the Lord is your strength.
(Nehemiah 8:10b)

Change Your Ways

In 1989, I had another dream. I dreamed that Ken was there beside me on the right-hand side of the bed, his side, and he was dead from alcoholism. So I reached for the phone which was on my side of the bed in my dream. In reality, the phone has always been on the other side, Ken's side of the bed. I dialed his dad and got a busy signal, and I kept dialing and dialing and could not get through.

I did not call the police or anyone else, but I felt I had to get up and go tell his dad first. I left Ken lying there, put my burgundy raincoat on over my nightgown and went to his dad's house. I walked up into the service porch and there was a UPS man there, a man who had gone to school with Ken from kindergarten. I told this man that I was Kenny's wife and I needed to talk to his dad.

The UPS man said, "Oh, you're Kenny's wife. How is he? You know, he's drank hard and he's played hard. How is he?"

I said, "Yes, and now he's dead!" and then I started screaming and screaming and couldn't stop. Ken had to wake me out of this dream. This was the third dream from which I had to literally be shaken awake. The first was the dream I had about Chuck dying and then he drowned, next it was when I dreamed Chuckie had leukemia and now this dream was about Ken.

I knew that God was telling me that I had to take a stand. This stand ultimately brought about Ken's departure. Approximately six months after Ken left, he asked me out to dinner and I went. As we were sitting at dinner, Ken said, "My dad sold his house."

Immediately I thought, "Oh, good, then that bad dream is not going to come about."

Then Ken said, "But he can't be out for another year because of taxes." I knew that if the dream was prophetic, it would have to happen while his dad still lived in the house. I had no idea what might happen to Ken during that one year period.

I went into deep prayer for Ken and asked God what was going to happen to Ken. I went to my Bible and God gave me a Scripture that stated God was going to repent (repent—Hebrew *nacham:* to change one's mind). Ken would live.

Therefore now amend your ways and your doings, and obey the voice of the Lord your God; and the Lord will repent him of the evil that he hath pronounced against you.
(Jeremiah 26:13)

Plans Fail For Lack Of Counsel

I read a letter written by a very honest alcoholic to a spouse, that went something like this:

I need help, but it may not be the kind of help you want to give. Don't lecture me, I won't listen.

Don't believe any promises I make to you about my drinking and don't believe everything I tell you. Don't cover up for me and don't make empty threats.

Don't lie for me, pay my bills, or meet my obligations.

Learn all you can about alcoholism. Use the truth you learn and talk to those who have overcome this terrible illness. They'll give you good counsel.

Plans fail for lack of counsel,
but with many advisers they succeed.
(Proverbs 15:22, NIV)

With Wings As Eagles

I had gone to two AA meetings when a woman asked me to go to one on a Saturday night. She was getting a divorce from her husband and she was hurting. I said, "Sure." This would be her first AA meeting, and she was hoping it would give her more understanding in relating to someone chemically dependent.

We met, went into the meeting and then I had to go wash my contacts. I came back and she was holding the roster, waiting for me, and she had signed it. In AA, you don't sign the roster if you're an Al-Anoner. I didn't want to embarrass her, so I wrote "Sophia—visitor." I was sure they would not call on me, but I was the first one called.

In my heart, I said, "Oh, Lord," but out of my mouth came these words, "Hi, my name is Sophia and I'm living with a practicing alcoholic and he's a turkey. But because of the twelve steps, and they're God-based, you guys are soaring like eagles. Thank you for sharing." Then I sat down.

The next morning, I taught Sunday School and then went into the service. A girl got up to sing special music and she said, "I have had my song picked out since last Wednesday, but I was awakened this morning at 6:00 a.m. And I know it was God, because no one wakes me up that early." Everyone laughed and then she continued, "So I know this song is for someone here. I hope it ministers to you." She then began to sing.

I had never heard the song before, but the words overwhelmed me. She sang, "Someday, I'll have more understanding. But right now, I will cling to God so I can soar like an eagle."

They that wait upon the Lord
shall renew their strength;
they shall mount up with wings as eagles;
they shall run, and not be weary;
and they shall walk, and not faint.
(Isaiah 40:31)

He Shall Call On Me

We began to sell Lotto tickets in our store in 1989. A lady came into the store shortly thereafter and cashed in a Lotto ticket with Ken. As he processed it, he noticed that a piece of paper popped out of the machine. "What is this?" he asked. A long line was waiting, the lady had moved on and Ken set the paper aside.

While closing that night, Ken ran across the paper again. After he studied it closely, he realized the lady had brought in a Lotto ticket with two wins on it—the $5.00 winner and a second combination of numbers winning $2,200.00. This was the first winning ticket our store had received. Ken came home and sat down on the foot of our bed, his face as white as a sheet. "Arlene, a lady came in tonight and won big, and I didn't handle it correctly. I have her winning ticket worth $2,200.00!"

"How did that happen, Ken?" I asked in amazement.

He looked at me in helpless anguish. He was very distraught, on the verge of upchucking. "What should we do now?" he said.

"I never saw this lady before, but there were two Mexican children with her. What am I going to do if she never comes in again, Arlene?"

Suddenly I knew the only thing we could do and I said, "Let's pray, Ken." So we knelt at the foot of the bed and prayed. We decided we would keep the ticket and maybe God would lead the lady into our store again before the six months deadline was up. If not, we would cash the ticket, put it in a savings account and let it draw interest while we tried to locate the winner.

Day after day, Ken looked anxiously for the woman to return, but he never saw her again. Nearly five and a half months later, I was sitting out front in my car waiting for Ken so we could go out to dinner when Ken suddenly came running out to another car. I thought to myself, "I wonder . . ."

Sure enough, Ken came over to our car and said excitedly, "I think I've found her—if these are the numbers she has always played. I can't believe it. If these are the same numbers, we've found her. I got her phone number, just in case." Even though the lady had bleached her hair and looked completely different, somehow Ken believed it must be her.

We went home and found that the numbers were indeed the same. The next day Ken had me call the lady to meet him at the store. She brought her husband with her and to their disbelief, Ken told her about the money that was hers. Then she told Ken that her husband had fallen off a roof and broken his back. It was right before Christmas and they had no money.

What a blessing! Just in the nick of time! God had honored Ken's honesty and our prayers for help.

He shall call upon me, and I will answer him:
I will be with him in trouble;
I will deliver him, and honour him.
(Psalm 91:15)

God Even Protects Him From Accidents

In 1989 I was going to Al-Anon and had also visited AA. While at one of the meetings, I picked up a little comic book about a couple who were in the throes of alcoholism. I told myself that I would keep it in my purse and when there was an appropriate time that I could give my complete attention to the little book, I would read it.

I asked my friend Linda to go to Modesto with me to visit my aunt and uncle. My Aunt Ethel had not felt all that up to par and Uncle Arlie (who I was named after) was not feeling too good, either. I told Linda that on the way back we would stop and get a shipment of meat at Victor Meats.

We got to the meat market late in the afternoon just before they closed. Linda wanted to come in with me, but I told her not to; I just had to give them the order and would be right back out. I went in, picked up an invoice and then walked back out to stand behind my van until a man came out to get the order. As I handed the invoice for the order to him, the little comic book flashed across my mind. It seemed like a perfect time to check it out.

I went around to the driver's door, opened it and got out the little book. I put my right foot up into the van and stood with my weight on my left leg. I think I had read about two pages when suddenly my head flew forward and backward and then forward and backward again. Then I went flying through the air and landed on my right side on the ground.

A big truck and trailer (eighteen-wheeler) had hit the back of our van, shoving it into me, throwing me into the air and away from the van. Linda had never taken off her seat belt and was sitting in the van.

The driver of the big truck was nearly frantic when he jumped out and ran around the van. His face flooded with relief when he saw me on the ground several feet away. He kept saying, "I thought she was under the van. I thought she was under the van. The last time I saw her, she was standing behind the van!"

This was a most unfortunate accident and the truck driver had in no way meant to jeopardize my life. But God, in His infinite timing, had already prepared a way for me to escape.

The good man does not escape all troubles—
he has them too. But the Lord helps him in
each and every one. God even protects him
from accidents.
(Psalm 34:19-20, TLB)

That Thou Mayest Live And Multiply

The choice I made to marry Ken brought me years of unhappiness, but it also caused me to make another choice: to become the repairer of the breach. God made man to commune with Him that man would have one-on-one relationship with Him. God saw that man was very lonely, and He gave him woman—not to trample upon, but to come into the oneness with God that man had at one time experienced. God made the woman to help the man meet his needs.

Sin came into the lives of man and woman. (Anything we have between our soul and our Savior is sin). Anything that we hold back and do not release to God becomes addiction which is bondage.

Isaiah 58:12 gives us guidelines that God wants us to follow if we are in a bondage situation—any bondage situation standing between our soul and our Savior—drugs, alcohol, verbal or physical abuse, Satanism, pornography, adultery, or fornication. When we acknowledge bondage, we say to it: No More!

God has called us to peace, and He frees us when we obey Him and cling to Him. This enables Him to free our mates from the generation garbage that has consumed and tried to destroy them. To be destroyed means that one will not receive eternal life. Salvation is a free gift, it is our choice. Salvation means Jesus Christ.

When we choose to receive Him, we are no longer in the bondage that has been and is destroying our lives. Life is precious and it is free.

God has called us to peace. Sometimes, in order to live in that peace, choices must be made. We find ourselves having to say "no" to those we love—no more until you get your life free from all the sin that is enslaving you. After 23 years of living in a bondage situation, I told Ken that he had to choose between alcohol or his family, for God had called us to peace.

Ken chose to leave our home on February 16, 1990.

See, I have set before thee this day life and
good, and death and evil;
in that I command thee this day to love the
Lord thy God, to walk in his ways, and to
keep his commandments and his statutes and
his judgments, that thou mayest live and
multiply:
and the Lord thy God shall bless thee
in the land whither thou goest to possess it.
(Deuteronomy 30:15-16)

Repairer Of The Breach

When Ken and I married, I vowed I would stay in the marriage "til death do us part," because I had taken him for better or for worse. But when he broke his vow to the sanctity of our marriage bed, I knew I was no longer under bondage to my vow. However, I made a choice to stay. I had been young and naive when I married him, and I didn't know I would someday be in the trouble I was now in, but I felt accountable to my marriage vows before God.

At that point, I believe I had two choices: to either get a divorce because the marriage bed had been broken or to become a repairer of the breach. I chose to do the latter, to become a repairer of the breach between my husband and God.

> *. . . Thou shalt be called the repairer of the breach, the restorer of paths to dwell in.*
> **(Isaiah 58:12b***)*

Isaiah 53

Two days after Ken left, a song came to me. I was able to finish the first and last verses, but I could not seem to finish the second verse. However, what I had written ministered deeply to me and I sang it constantly.

A year later, I took my two youngest daughters, Julie and Tiffany, and two of their friends to Lodi Lake. On the way to the lake, we each took a turn choosing a song to sing. After awhile, it was my turn. I said, "Julie, how about that song that Jesus and I wrote?"

She replied, "All right, Mama." I could tell by her voice that she was only trying to appease me. We started singing and got to the words, "Isaiah 43," Julie sang, "Isaiah 53."

I said, "Julie, you know it's Isaiah 43. Why did you say Isaiah 53?"

"I don't know, Mama."

And I thought to myself, "I think I do." We never did finish singing the song, but I could hardly wait until I got home so I could read Isaiah 53. What could it be? Could I have heard the wrong chapter or was this just a coincidence? I knew that Isaiah 43 had helped me through the waters and through the fire.

Later, when I got my Bible out, I understood. It was not a coincidence. I had needed Isaiah 43 at the time the Lord had begun the song in me. But to finish it, I needed the real reason the song was written. The song was never intended to be written about what had happened to me. It was to be written about our Savior who died on the Cross and freed us by every stripe He took for our sins.

After a year of trying to complete its words, in one minute, the song was finished. I wondered why the Lord had me repeat the last stanza three times. I believe it is because it takes three times for some things to really sink into our spirits. Jesus truly does give us freedom when we accept Him as Isaiah prophesied.

Free To Be Me
I don't have to think about that garbage anymore
I don't have to listen to that garbage anymore
I don't have to be insane and my life in misery
Praise God! Praise God! I'm Free!

I'm soaring like an eagle now, Isaiah 53!
I'm soaring like an eagle now, His stripes have set me free
I'm soaring like an eagle now, salvation lifted me
Praise God! Praise God! I'm Free!

Take your life, live it now, our God He loves you so
Take your life, live it now, our God He loves you so
Take your life, live it now, our God He loves you so
Praise God! I'm Free! I'm me!

To appoint unto them that mourn in Zion,
to give unto them beauty for ashes, the oil of joy for
mourning, the garment of praise for the spirit of
heaviness; that they might be called trees of
righteousness, a planting of the Lord that he might
be glorified.
(Isaiah 61:3)

Strengthen Me

Right after Ken left, I purchased a new phone because Ken had taken our phone and thrown it at me. So I purchased a little blue phone for my room and Julie told me that she had plugged in the phone for me. I thanked her and went into my bedroom and saw that she had placed the phone on my side of the bed, the same side as it had been in the dream about Ken being dead. I yelled, "Julie, get that phone off there!"

She was shaken, but said, "Mom, I just wanted to help you and please you."

I pulled myself under control and said, "I'm sorry, Julie, but that is where the phone was in my dream about your daddy."

My soul is weary with sorrow;
strengthen me according to your word.
(Psalm 119:28, NIV)

I Will Heal Him

Six months after Ken left, I was at a meeting conducted by a man who had also had problems in a marriage. Afterwards there was an altar call and I practically ran to the altar to receive from God. I heard, *"Let him go. He will be healed."*

I said, "Oh, Lord. You can heal him any time, anywhere—you can heal him right now." I heard again, *"Let him go. I will heal him."*

Later, I had a dream that I could not remember when I awoke. All I knew was that I could hear the word "relinquish." "Relinquish" means to let go. This is what God wants us to do to repair the breach: let go. The only way to be used by God is to let go and let God have His way in our lives.

Let go means for us to relinquish our "clinging vine syndrome" and cling to God, our Father, instead. We must talk to our heavenly Father and listen to Him if He says to let go and separate ourselves from the trauma we find ourselves in.

And Jesus said unto him,
I will come and heal him.
(Matthew 8:7)

Between You And Your God

After Ken left, I was drinking pots of coffee. But I was set free from coffee in December of 1990. The following year, in the month of May, I had a dream. In the dream, I was in Pansy's (Ken's mother) house which is next door to Turner and Marie's (Ken's brother and sister-in-law) house. Turner and Ken were there, but Marie was not. A young woman and my children were there, too. I went to Ken, kissed him goodbye and left the house.

Once outside, I heard screaming coming from Turner and Marie's house. I ran into their house and found four men inside, three of them shirtless, fighting with each other. They were all drunk and didn't even know what they were fighting about.

When I came in, they stopped fighting and looked at me. For some reason, they seemed to think I was sent by the law. Marie said to them, "No, this is my sister-in-law, Kenny's wife."

The men suddenly settled down and wanted to talk. One man said, "I want to quit drinking so bad, but I just can't."

Another man said, "I want to stop, too, but I can't either."

I said, "If you really want to, this is how you do it." The men just looked at me. "The reason people don't really stop doing what they are doing is because part of them enjoys it so much and that part can't let go. The reason I know that is because one day I said, 'God, please let me stop drinking coffee.' And when you truly desire to give your whole self to God, then

He will deliver you from whatever you're trying to break away from." And then, in my dream, I related my exact experience that I had with an addiction to coffee.

I like the smell of coffee, the flavor of coffee—I loved everything about coffee. But its side effects were bad. Coffee made me shake, made me nervous and made me, in essence, a different person toward other human beings. I was just not myself when I drank coffee. It also made lumps in my breasts and I knew that caffeine was linked to cancer. I wanted to stop, but I just couldn't seem to do it.

Although we were separated, Ken got me an expresso coffee maker for my birthday and Julie was to wrap it. I did not accept the coffee maker, saying, "If I can't have you, I don't want anything of yours. Besides that, I quit drinking coffee." I turned to go and as I did, I said, "Oh, God, that is a lie between you and me. I've tried to quit drinking coffee, but now, Lord, *forgive me* and take coffee from me. Thank you, Lord."

For the next seven days I found it easy to drink no coffee. I was on my way to meet a friend for a church outing and suddenly I said, "Lord, I didn't say decaf coffee! I think it would be all right if I had a cup of decaf."

When I got to the restaurant where I was supposed to meet my friend, Char, we both sat down in a booth and the waitress came to take our order. I asked if they had decaf, and she said she had just made a fresh pot. I got so excited, I could hardly wait as I said, "Okay, please bring me a fresh cup of decaf."

Char was not aware of my complete surrender to God with coffee as I had not shared it with anyone.

When the waitress brought our drinks, I quickly picked up the cup of decaf. It was steaming up like it was calling to me. I started to take a drink and suddenly, from the very bottom of my stomach, I became terribly sick. I was so nauseous, it was like having morning sickness. I couldn't help myself from gagging.

Char said, "Arlene, what in the world is the matter? Are you all right?"

When I was finally able to compose myself, I began to laugh. Coffee was no longer a part of my life. When I had truly committed my whole self in desiring to be free from coffee, God had delivered me.

Anything between our soul and our Savior is sin— anything (coffee, alcohol, sex)—anything we hold there is addiction.

*"But your iniquities have separated between you and your God, and your sins have hid His face from you, that He will not **hear**."*

(Isaiah 59:2)

*If my people, who are called by my name, will humble themselves and pray and seek my face and turn from their wicked ways, then will I **hear** from heaven and will forgive their sin and will heal their land.*

(2 Chronicles 7:14)

And He Saved Them Out Of Their Distress

Ken was undergoing many changes. He had changed his outward appearance and He had bought a little BMW. One day I was at the home of a real woman of prayer, Sister Gorman, and as we were praying for Ken, she suddenly said, "Oh, no, Lord. Don't let that happen. No, Lord." When we finished praying, she told me that she had seen Ken in a bad accident and that she had prayed against it.

Sure enough, in 1991, Ken wrecked his little car. But God was true to His Word and Ken was not killed. There was $19,000.00 worth of damage.

God was trying to get Ken's attention and He did! But Ken's rebellion kept him in his bondage.

Then they cried to the Lord in their trouble,
and he saved them from their distress.
(Psalm 107:13, NIV)

Train Up A Child

My friend Martha and I went to a large church with Kimberly and Joshua John, my one year old grandson. Martha was holding Joshua on my left and Kimberly was sitting on my right. The preacher prayed for quite a lengthy time and I opened my left eye to check on Joshua. At the same time, Joshua turned and looked at Kimberly who had raised her left hand to God as she praised Him. Joshua then raised his face upward and lifted his left hand in praise to God. What a thrill for me!

The Scriptures say to train up a child in the way he should go. "Lord, what is your way?" we ask. The Scriptures give us guidance as to how we train our children by examples such as Lamentations 3:41 where we are told to lift up our heart with our hands unto God in the heavens. As always, every answer we ever need can be found in God's holy Word.

Yes, Joshua was only one, but in his eyes I could see praise and adoration as he felt the communion that God intended for His children.

Train up a child in the way he should go
and when he is old he will not turn from it.
(Proverbs 22:6, NIV)

Pour out your heart like water in the presence
of the Lord. Lift up your hands to him for the
lives of your children.
(Lamentations 2:19, NIV)

Thou Makest Me Dwell In Safety

About six months after Ken left, I was hurting so bad one night I thought I would die. I went into the utility room every night to pray, so the children would not hear me cry. This particular night, I just couldn't get relief from the pain I was feeling inside. All I could do was pray, read the Bible and praise God.

Suddenly that night, as I sat there with my eyes closed tight, I began to rock back and forth. Somehow I felt that I was in Noah's Ark.

"Oh, Lord," I cried, "I'm in Noah's Ark, aren't I?" I had no idea why I felt that way, but it seemed like I was in a floating cocoon. I was so relieved and excited. My pain was gone.

The next day, I related my experience to my friend, Holly, and she said, "Arlene, don't you know that Noah's Ark represents safety?"

*I will both lay me down in peace, and sleep
for thou, Lord, only makest me dwell in
safety.*
(Psalm 4:8)

Ah Lord God

When Ken had been gone for two years, I was in the kitchen when I suddenly doubled over with anguish. I bent over to my knees and cried out, "Ah, Lord God!" But as I came up, I was singing, "Thou hast made the heavens and the earth by Thou great power!"

That very night when I was reading God's Word, the Book of Jeremiah, I found out that Jeremiah cried out to God with the exact same words, "Ah, Lord God!"

Ah, Lord God! behold, thou hast made
the heaven and the earth by thy great power
and stretched out arm, and there is nothing
too hard for thee.
(Jeremiah 32:17)

The Desires Of Your Heart

One day in August of 1991, I went to the prayer meeting before evening church. After prayer, there was a good message on "God Will Give You The Desire Of Your Heart."

I went forward to pray for my family and put them on the altar. When the preacher came to me, I said, "I want a boldness I have never had."

Before church I had spoken with a brother in the Lord, telling him that I felt so humiliated. He replied, "But, Arlene, God was humiliated many times. He was beaten, He was spit upon." I realized that I had a long way to go before I truly portrayed a son of God.

During the evening service, the pastor's sermon was "A Desire Was Great," speaking of the olden days when people used to put their desires on the altar. Then there was more prayer. I had written a note to my friend sitting with me which said, "My desire is that Ken be saved."

Right after I wrote the note, the pastor said, "Now put your desire on the altar."

I opened the note again and wrote, "Father, forgive him, he knows not what he is doing." Without showing the note to my friend, I went forward and put it on the altar.

The following day, my friend Holly, said she had been invited to see a prophetess, Charlotte Potter, and asked me to go with her.

The meeting was wonderful. Charlotte was anointed and the Word flowed from her like a water

faucet. As she was preaching, suddenly she stopped
and pointed towards me in the middle of one of the
back rows. She said, "Honey, can I pray for you?"
I rose from my seat and went towards her, and she
prophesied the answer to my desire from the night
before.

"You know what I hear God saying? Be real strong
and have a real good courage, because down on the
inside—*what you're longing for, what you want from
Him, what you want from Jesus (not just from life)*—
Jesus is going to give it to you. The Lord said that
He's going to strengthen you.

"He's going to give you an understanding. He's
going to open your mind and you are going to really,
absolutely know His voice. You're going to know
the slightest whisper to the loudest shout that God
gives you; and when He gives it to you, it's going to
be very beautiful. God says don't listen to any man.
Don't listen to negative thinking. Don't listen to
anything that would come to try to stop what God is
preparing for you. The Lord is going to bless you."

*Delight thyself also in the Lord
and He will give you the desires
of your heart.*
(Psalm 37:4, NIV)

Be Strong And Courageous

Shortly after the meeting I went to my sister and brother-in-law's cabin in the mountains. Then, I took out my Bible and asked God to give me a word from Him. I turned to 1 Chronicles where God was telling David, "Just like I told Moses, David, be strong and of good courage." I felt those words were for me, too.

Charlotte's first prophecy to me began with those same words, "Be strong and of good courage." I began to realize how important everyone is in the sight of God. No one is left out. God's Word was for Moses, David, Joshua and me.

Be strong and of good courage;
dread not, nor be dismayed.
(1 Chronicles 22:13b)

Neither is there respect of persons with him.
(Ephesians 6:9b)

Steps Of A Good Man

I later attended another meeting of Charlotte Potter's, and she gave me the following prophecy from the Lord: *I'm going to meet a financial need, an immediate financial need.* I did not understand what this meant. However, I knew we could always use financial help. But I continued to ponder the meaning.

The next week, I discovered that I had somehow neglected to make tax pre-payments to the State Board of Equalization. The amount totalled $6,000.00 and I was facing not only that pre-payment, but a large penalty as well. At first my mind jumped with questions, "Lord, how did this happen? Why did this happen?" After I had prayed, I was a little calmer and began to say, "Well, Lord, it's just money. No one has died. I'm not going to worry about this."

That night I continued to pray that God would give me understanding. The next morning, I realized what had happened. I looked at my calendar and sure enough, one week before the first pre-payment was due, my son went to jail for spousal problems. With everything that was going on, I had blocked out the issue of the pre-payment. The following month, the week before the pre-payment was due, my son went to court again. Once more I somehow blocked out the payment.

"Lord, what do I do now?" I asked. At once I knew. I got my calendar and checkbook and went to the State Board of Equalization.

When the lady behind the counter asked, "Mrs. Grant, what can we do for you?"

I replied, "I need a miracle." Then I proceeded to tell her about my memory blocks after making these pre-payments for twenty years. She took down all the information and I gave her the $6,000.00 in overdue tax pre-payments. She said the State Board would let me know what the penalty would be.

I left the building, thanking God that the matter was now firmly in His hands. Finally I got a letter from the State Board. When I opened it, the verdict was "no penalty."

God had miraculously fulfilled His prophetic Word to me.

The steps of a good man are ordered by the Lord: and he delighteth in his way. Though he fall, he shall not be utterly cast down: for the Lord upholdeth him with his hand.
(Psalm 37:23-24)

Dressed In White

In a vision dream, Julie put on her pajamas and climbed into her bed. As she settled down for the night, suddenly her Grandpa Leon appeared to her in a dream and Julie cried out, "Grandpa, Grandpa!" She told me later, "It didn't look like Grandpa, but somehow I knew it was him." A young boy was with him, also.

Then her grandfather said to her, "Get dressed, Julie, I want to take you somewhere."

"Where do you want to take me, Grandpa?"

"Just get dressed, Julie."

In Julie's own words, this is the scenario that began to unfold:

I got dressed and Grandpa took me to my mother's room. She was lying curled up in almost a fetal position, crying in a low whimper. Then Grandpa and the boy took me to a party where Daddy was, but Daddy wasn't having any fun.

Then they took me to a place that had a very large gate with jeweled handles on it, but the gate opened by itself. The streets were gold, but you could see through them. It was like I could see clouds below the streets, like heaven was suspended between clouds. The clouds above were light blue with a purple hue. I had never seen clouds like these before.

Many beautiful trees and beautiful flowers were all around us, there was only beauty everywhere. The houses were large mansions with jewels. And then he took me to a street with a sign that said, "Grant's Road." I said, "Grandpa, will all the Grants be here?"

He replied, "Yes, all the Grants."

"Even my Daddy?"

"Yes, Julie, even your daddy."

Then I turned to the boy who was with Grandpa and asked, "Who are you?"

He said, "I'm your brother Chuckie. Julie, I'm here with you always. I love you."

I turned back to my Grandpa, who said, "We have to go back now, Julie."

"No, Grandpa, I want to stay here with you. I never want to go back."

Chuckie said, "You have to go back. Our mother needs you, Julie. We have to take you back." And they took me back and Grandpa tucked me in bed just like he used to do.

The next morning, when Julie woke up, she was completely dressed. Julie's experience seemed to answer so many of her questions. Her grandfather had accepted Jesus on his death bed and Julie had wondered if he had truly made it to heaven. She had also wondered if we would know our loved ones when we reached heaven. Julie was comforted and reassured by all she had seen: the golden streets, the great beauty, many wonderful butterflies, and the singing of birds.

Julie said later that everyone she saw, as she walked those golden streets, had on wedding attire. The women wore beautiful wedding dresses and the men were wearing white tuxedos with ruby buttons and ruby cuff links. It seemed as if everyone was getting married. And each one appeared to be singing to themselves, as if they were constantly singing praise songs. They were not embarrassed or ashamed to be doing so.

They will walk with me, dressed in white, for they are worthy. He who overcomes will, like them, be dressed in white. I will never blot out his name from the book of life.
(Revelation 3:4-5 NIV)

Until I Make Thine Enemies Thy Footstool

This August 19, 1991, prophecy from Charlotte Potter was answered in part the night when I heard the Lord's words regarding Ken, *"Challenge him."*

"You know what I hear the Lord say? 'I am going to make your enemies your footstool.' Everything that has been troubling and plaguing you, standing steadfast and immovable against anything you can do to go forth and accomplish and achieve, the Lord says He is going to make your enemies your footstool.

"There is a moment coming when you're going to rejoice; there is a moment coming when the light of Christ is going to shine so strong from your countenance because of the glory of God and the mind of the Lord that He gives to you and the will of an almighty God that is going to be manifested through you. Watch and see. Very soon, I'm not talking about six months from now, I'm not talking about a year from now. *I'm not even talking a week from now.* God is moving now!

"Very soon you are going to see an answer. It is absolutely just like a little spark of fire smoldering in smoke. You'll look and say, 'It would take a big wind to get it really going. It looks like it's dying out.'

"But God says all He needs is just a little breeze, just a little thing, and flames can come up just as high as they can be, burning on nothing but God Himself. You mark the Word of the Lord. For you, He is going to move; for you, He's going to give you an insight. He's going to give you a living faith and you're going

*to be amazed at the <u>words that are going to come on
the inside and when you act upon them, you're going
to see the glory of the Lord.</u> Soon, your enemies are
going to be your footstool.*

In six days a further answer came. Ken was at my
door wanting to see and be with me. He did not come
to see the children or to discuss work. He expounded
on our lives. God was moving.

I have had to put a lot of things under my feet—or
my footstool.

> *The Lord said unto my Lord, Sit thou at my
> right hand, until I make thine enemies thy
> footstool.*
> **(Psalm 110:1)**

So Shall Ye Be Established

After returning from Charlotte Potter's meeting on Monday, August 19, 1991, I was working in the kitchen. Ken had taken the kids to the fair. It was nearing time for him to bring them home when I heard the words, *"Challenge him."*

I questioned, "Challenge him, Lord?" The first page for this book flashed in my mind along with Charlotte Potter's prophecy about the experiences I've had. I said, "Okay, Lord."

I got the book and put the tape of the prophecy on the tape player. Just then, Ken walked in. I said, "You know this lady that I told you about, the one I've seen twice that I believe Jesus speaks through?" He looked at me and nodded. "Ken, if I can prove to you that Jesus speaks through her, would you go to see her?"

Ken replied, "Arlene, if you can prove that to me without a shadow of a doubt, I'll go."

So I said, "You know that you haven't read any of the book that I'm writing, but you told me years ago that you would give me a thousand dollars to get it published."

"Yeah, so what is it?"

"Ken, listen to this." I read him the first page of my manuscript and then turned on the tape of Charlotte Potter's prophecy of August 15, 1991, which said:

Experiences you've had, ones that have been so treasured by you, Jesus has made known and given as treasures that you hold in here through that precious

Word. But it is not just the Word, it is the <u>manifestation</u> of it that you have seen Him do. He's answered your prayers many times.

He has caused things to turn around and change, things that looked impossible, even when somebody said to you, "Oh, don't be foolish, believing like that." But you still did and God proved himself as God and, honey, you weren't made ashamed. You had your answer.

There's everything for you and everything preparing itself today and everything that looks like a darkness or a bondage, you're going to see it as a marvelous light. You're going to see it in the eyes of Jesus Christ. And He's going to let you look right in the very situation to understand the core and the root of it. And, honey, what you've seen in the past, you're going to see far greater in the future and you're going to be able to help a lot of people and a lot of souls to turn around from what is binding and holding them. Thank you, Jesus, thank you, Lord.

Ken became very angry and said, "How much did you pay her, Arlene? Just how much did you pay her?"

"Ken, you know I didn't pay her anything. Now, will you go and see her?"

He looked at me and said, "I told you I would, didn't I?"

I said softly, "Thank you, Lord."

This prophecy stated that the experiences I have had would help many people out of bondage. The book I had been writing for years described experiences I have had in bondage situations. The prophecy shows that God speaks through man.

Believe in the Lord your God, so shall ye be established; believe his prophets, so shall ye prosper.
(2 Chronicles 20:20b)

For the testimony of Jesus is the spirit of prophecy.
(Revelation 19:10)

He Makes His Steps

On August 25, 1991, exactly six days after Charlotte Potter had prophesied, Ken did go to the Prayer Center and she prophesied to him. As she spoke, Ken said his head tingled and then his body tingled all over. No one in the Prayer Center knew anything about Ken. God speaks so gently in front of other people. This is the prophecy that Ken received:

"I can see some stepping stones being put down . . . little ones, I don't see big ones. If you go off the stepping stones, you're in the mud, you're in trouble. I see this person looking up while stepping on them, without looking down.

"Nobody knows anyone like Jesus knows you. If you were to speak what you feel and what you have in your heart . . . what you would love to accomplish and see happen, no one could really understand. But there is One who does and very soon, very soon, you are going to see your answer."

If the Lord delights in a man's way, he makes his steps firm; though he stumble, he will not fall, for the Lord upholds him with his hand.
(Psalm 37:23-24, NIV)

Be Still

God wanted me to slow down. I dreamed one night that I drove into a gas station and a child was pumping gas into a milk carton. Instead of stopping him, I went into the store to find out who had sold gas to a child. Then I went back out and the child was gone.

The feeling I remember from the dream was that the gas had exploded and I was too late. I was too worried about everything else instead of the safety of lives and the salvation of souls. I have since slowed down in my life, paused to reflect, and have taken a second look at many things.

The following is an article that ministered to me. With warm gratitude to the writer for her permission to reprint:

By Clare Miseles

God has not created one, two or three kinds of turtles, but fifty different kinds. He placed them on land, in the desert and in the sea. He also made them slowpokes. Land turtles are slower than molasses in January. Sea turtles can swim with moderate speed, but they don't set any records.

How really slow do turtles travel? Well, let's make some comparisons. The snake slithers along the ground at two miles per hour, which is far from speedy. The goldfish doubles that speed at the rate of four miles per hour. Where does that leave the turtle? Poking along at one-tenth of a mile an hour!

Does that bother the turtle? Is that why his head is drawn into his shell and stays there? No way! The turtle, which God put on earth even before He created Adam and Eve, doesn't mind a bit. He keeps moving on slowly without even caring to watch the rest of the world go by.

Yes, the turtle is quite content to be what he is— slow. He accepts himself as God made him. He doesn't try to be pretty like a bird or strong like a bull. He doesn't spend his life wishing he were someone else. He's just happy being a turtle.

That isn't all that pleases the turtle. God has blessed him with a long, long life. The goldfish dies quickly; the snake doesn't live long either. Even the dog and cat rarely make it to 16 or 17. Horses live usually until the age of 25. The gorilla never reaches 50. Ah, but the turtle, the slowpoke turtle, lives on and on to the ripe old age of 100, 125 or even 150 years! And he doesn't spend one day out of all those years complaining about who God made him to be, or feeling sorry for himself. We can learn a lesson from this content slowpoke—don't dislike yourself because you're not like someone else, but accept yourself— God loves you.

Be still, and know that I am God.
(Psalm 46:10a)

Sing To The Lord

I love you, Lord,
I praise you, Lord,
I thank you, Lord!

What a trio, what a combination, what a miracle. True freedom!

These three phrases gave me strength to endure. This has sustained me even when all seemed dark. Chuckie and I wrote a song on the way to the hospital and I used his first stanza and then I combined the rest.

Praise and Worship
I love you Father God, I love you so much
I love you Father God, I love you so much
I love you Father God, thank you for your touch
I love you Father God, I love you so much.
(Kimberly and Ken Jr. would then sing:)
Doo-doot, doo-doot, doo-doot!

I praise you Lord Jesus, I praise you so much
I praise you Lord Jesus, I praise you so much
I praise you Lord Jesus, for living in us
I praise you Lord Jesus, I praise you so much.
Doo-doot, doo-doot, doo-doot!

I thank you Holy Spirit, I thank you so much
I thank you Holy Spirit, I thank you so much
I thank you Holy Spirit, for your love toward us
I thank you Holy Spirit, I thank you so much.
Doo-doot, doo-doot, doo-doot!

Kimberly was five years old when we lost Chuckie, and Ken Jr. was three.

Sing to the Lord a new song; sing to the Lord, all the earth. Sing to the Lord, praise his name; proclaim his salvation day after day.
(Psalm 96:1-2, NIV)

I will praise the name of God with a song, and will magnify him with thanksgiving. This also shall please the Lord...
(Psalm 69:30-31)

I will give thee thanks in the great congregation: I will praise thee among much people.
(Psalm 35:18)

Seven times a day do I praise thee because of thy righteous judgments.
(Psalm 119:164)

The Confidence We Have

There were many things in the prophecy given to me by Charlotte Potter on

January 12, 1992 that no one knew except God.

"Arlene, I am moving this day and this hour on your behalf. I am moving in a mighty way, greater than you can imagine. I am moving in My will and your life and this is what you want and what you asked for. I am moving at the very root of all things that are yours and all things that belong to you. I am turning things around and though it is not seen or felt, you shall see it soon, and you shall know of a truth that when I am finished, it shall be well established.

"And I say to you, my daughter, what your heart cries for, the love you have in your heart and your trust in Me, it is going to be well rewarded, it already is rewarded, but you're going to see the end of that reward and that is going to be everything a mighty God could give to you. You mark My word, my daughter, I have led you and I have guided you down through the years. I have led you in your thoughts and in your feelings. I have led you and you have obeyed.

"Sometimes you wondered if you had obeyed Me, sometimes you wondered if you had done My will. Sometimes you wondered if you had made a mistake. And sometimes you listened to the voice of man and thought, "Well, I can't try that."

"And you were right. The times that things went dead wrong inside and the times that you could not move, the times that there wasn't light or life and you stood still and prayed, the times you were so careful with your words, it was all of Me.

"I have led you, I have guided you, and I have directed you toward a great victory. I have led you and guided your life not just for the victory that you will have in your life, but what you will have in My life that is in you. You will know and understand many things. You will see the revelation to be able to help another soul. You are one who will be able to help a troubled *heart,* a troubled *mind*, a troubled *spirit,* because you've been troubled yourself.

"You will know how to impart peace, you will know how to cause a soul to come into the kingdom of God. I am going to give you a ministry, a ministry of healing the hearts, healing the minds and souls and spirits. You will have a ministry that will flow in the beauty of all that is inside of you that has been buried through heartbreak and sorrow, but is alive and showing itself and manifesting itself just in small measures.

"But the moment is coming when it will be a river of life, and the moment is coming when it will flow, and the moment is coming when it will be free and the moment is coming when it will be beauty. You shall cause many hearts to be healed and cause many souls to turn around to God and *many marriages to be restored.*

"This is my will for your life, and all the heartbreak you have suffered and all the sorrow you have gone through is going to turn to joy. It is going to turn to joy and you're going to know a joy of soul saving and thanksgiving for everything you have been through for My perfect will to be done, saith thy God."

As this anointed prophetess uttered these last words, she immediately began to praise God over and over for what He had spoken through her.

This is the confidence we have in approaching God: that if we ask anything according to his will, he hears us.
(1 John 5:14, NIV)

God Shall Send Forth His Mercy

Early in 1992, I invited Ken's mother to go with Julie, Tiffany and me to a small town just above San Francisco to spend the night. On the way I encountered the first of some very bad curves. Mom and I looked at each other, and I said, "I've got to slow down!" I did. The speed limit was thirty-five miles an hour. About three miles farther, a policeman pulled me over on this winding road and told me I had been clocked as going over forty-five miles an hour. "I don't understand that." I said.

He said, "Well, I have it on the radar."

I got back in my car and said, "Mom, I don't understand that because there is no way I could have driven this big van around those curves at that rate of speed. We would have had a wreck!"

She said, "I don't think we were going forty-five miles an hour, honey."

When we went home, we returned the same way because I wanted to go over my tracks and try to determine what had transpired. I knew in my heart that something was wrong. I got the ticket in the mail saying that I was exceeding the speed limit and the amount of my fine. I still didn't feel in my heart that I had broken the law.

If you get a ticket more than one hundred miles from home, you can mail a written affidavit. I wrote a letter and signed it under penalty of perjury. Then I typed up a letter for Ken's mother and she signed it. We sent the letters to court along with the money they requested. The court sent it back saying that the case was dismissed and the charge was dropped.

God doesn't want us to just sit back because we're Christians and watch the world go on around us with people accusing us. When we know that we are right, we should follow through. In the Bible where God said that He gave one man five talents and another man two talents and yet another man one talent. Each man was held accountable for everything that he was given. God wants us to know that we are held accountable for everything that He puts before us.

He shall send from heaven,and save me
from the reproach of him that would swallow
me up. Selah. God shall send forth his mercy
and his truth
(Psalm 57:3)

Joyful In Hope

I was in deep depression, crying, praying, pleading with God. I would not even get up in the morning. As I lay curled up in my bed during the day, looking toward the sliding glass door, I had a vision of Ken at the foot of my bed. He said that he had just come from being with Turner and Marie at Lake Tahoe.

Then I seemed to have another vision within the vision and I saw Turner and Marie leaving a motel in the mountains. I lay there, not really caring what I was seeing. And then Ken turned towards me again and he said, "You know, Arlene, our children are beautiful."

I thought to myself, "He wants me to respond!" I already knew our children were beautiful and I wondered what it was that he wanted from me. The only thing we had in common was our children. I had such a sense of not caring, I even said to myself, "I don't care." What a wonderful feeling.

Then I slowly began to get out of my bed. And this time, I deliberately arose from my side of the bed. I went to the bedroom door, and Ken also moved toward the bedroom door. The sudden ringing of my telephone brought me back to the awareness of my sunlight-filled bedroom.

I realize that when Ken does come home, I will be able to believe him—he will be well established. God is changing him and doing a new work in him. God gave me this vision to sustain me during the tribulation period. He always continues to guide.

Rejoicing in hope: patient in tribulation; continuing instant in prayer.
(Romans 12:12)

When We Pray

Something happens when we pray
that doesn't when we don't.
Will you up and miss a chance
by deciding that you won't?

When the burden of our circumstance
seems impossible to bear,
We think the last thing we want to do
is stop and say a prayer!

We're so desperate for solutions,
for answers we grasp in vain.
We don't care about the how or why
we just want relief from all our pain.

We are pummeled by adversity,
at our jugular, anxiety holds a knife.
While terror and deception
gingerly plot how to take our life.

We are frightened by these shadows,
our perceptions of the harm that
they may bring.
However, we can choose to change our
focus which will neutralize their sting.

It's time to take a stand
and learn how to defeat our foe,
cast your gaze upon Our Lord
and to Him let your trials go.

I witness many miracles
as I travel life's winding way,
the only things He asks of me
are that I love, trust and pray.

—by Eugene S. Davis

Used with kind permission.
Complete poem and information about other
poetry by Eugene S. Davis may be obtained
by writing to:
PO Box 162875, Sacramento, CA 95816

E-mail siloam@pacbell.net

Your Confidence . . . Has Great Reward

As I had prayed, God had shown me that my life has been a furnace of affliction. *"Behold, I have refined thee, but not with silver; I have chosen thee in the furnace of affliction"* (Isaiah 48:10). Then on March 1, 1992, God gave me a prophecy after I had been fasting for three days and it said: I am going to triumph!

"Arlene, I hear God say, Don't ever give up. Don't ever stop in what you believe in. Do what God puts in your heart, because *you're going to triumph.* He says, the day is coming, the hour is coming, when you are going to see so clearly and when you do, every pain and every heartbreak and every sorrow will be gone out of you.

"You're going to shine for Jesus and you're going to cause a lot of hearts in broken people to be healed. You watch, you're going to be a great light, a great witness to them. Your enduring is going to be well rewarded and great blessing is coming your way."

Cast not away your confidence,
which hath great recompence of reward.
(Hebrews 10:35)

184

The Kind Of Fasting I Have Chosen

On March 8, 1992, the Spirit of the Lord burned within me to start a fasting book and a prayer journal at Charlotte Potter's meetings. I am so grateful to God for giving me the desire to start these journals. The fasting book has put discipline into my daily walk, both physically and spiritually. The prayer journal has given purpose and meaning to my fasting.

The fasting book has a two-fold purpose: the making of a commitment to God to fast one's food or one's pleasures—either way—giving oneself one hundred percent to God. Isaiah 58 relates to fasting and verse 3 relates to pleasures: *"We have fasted before you, they say. Why aren't you impressed? Why don't you see our sacrifices? Why don't you hear our prayers? We have done much penance, and you don't even notice it! I'll tell you why! Because you are living in evil pleasure even while you are fasting, and you keep right on oppressing your workers"* (TLB).

The fasting book is broken up into six-hour increments of commitment: 12 A.M. to 6 A.M., 6 A.M. to 12 P.M., 12 P.M. to 6 P.M., and 6 P.M. to 12 A.M.

Someone is fasting and praying at different hours of every day and night. We put no names in the book, instead we enter a symbol (a sign, a tiny drawing, something that has meaning only to ourselves and to God). This is our commitment to God. Everything in the fasting book is between a person and God. The six-hour commitment each person makes becomes their personal time of praying and talking to God, as the Holy Spirit prompts them, for those in the prayer journal.

The fasting book turned my life around. When I began to commit my pleasures to God, my nails were all bitten off, sometimes bleeding down past the quick. I was an addicted nail biter for as long as I could remember. Also, I would not take vitamins. I bought them, but they sat on a shelf. I made a commitment to God that I would fast my nail biting and take my vitamins. In three months, my nails grew hard and long. I did this unto God.

My right hip and leg still hurt so much from the accident, so I made a commitment to faithfully do all my exercises and physical therapy unto God. I looked in my Bible for references on exercise. In Biblical days, men always traveled by foot! We don't even want to walk from an outer row parking space at the mall. I now walk every day for half an hour and do the exercises my therapist gave me.

Luke 21:34 says: "And take heed to yourselves, lest at any time your hearts be overcharged with surfeiting, and drunkenness, and cares of this life, and so that day come upon you unawares." Surfeiting means immoderate indulgence or disgust caused by excess. Overcharged is what we do on our credit cards so we can have more. Surfeiting is anything we do to indulge in excess. I have determined for myself that there are certain indulgences I will not partake of anymore. For example, I have chosen not to eat sweets after 6:00 P.M. In fact, whenever I eat anything sweet, I walk it off.

I have begun to drink eight cups of water a day as a commitment unto God. I never saw my parents drink water, so I didn't either. But I have made a commitment to God to change that. I make my bed and I clean my house as a commitment to God. This tool, the fasting book, has brought commitment and discipline into my life. I know I can't do these things on my own, for I have already failed trying it that way. But I can do anything to the Lord who strengthens me. Colossians 3:23 tells us: "And whatsoever ye do, do it heartily, as to the Lord, and not unto men."

Before, in my life, the spotlight was always on Ken's problems and my problems instead of the world around me and all of its suffering. Can you relate to that? Today, when I commit these things to God, I pray for everyone, every prayer request, in the prayer journal. This gets my mind off my problems and situations.

It is possible to give away and become richer! It is also possible to hold on too tightly and lose everything. Yes, the liberal man shall be rich! By watering others, he waters himself. (Proverbs 11:24-25).

People cannot manipulate God, but they can pray. The prayer journal has many deep, dramatic desires and needs in it. It is written proof of the realization of many that they have come to their end, knowing they can do nothing in themselves. When they accept this, then they can hear the truth of Luke 18:27: "The things which are impossible with men are possible with God."

Try this. It works. Fast it to God.

Is not this the fast I have chosen?
To loose the bands of wickedness, to undo the
heavy burdens, and to let the oppressed go
free, and that ye break every yoke?
(Isaiah 58:6)

187

Then Shall They Fast

November 9, 1992: Today I woke up and said, "Lord, should I start a fast?" and I heard "No." I thought that it was just me, but I went on about my way. Later, I asked again, "Lord, do you think I should start a fast?" and again I heard "No." The very first prophecy that Charlotte ever gave me was that I would know His voice. I would know His slightest whisper and the loudest shout He would give to me.

About an hour later, Ken was at my door and wanted to take me out to breakfast. Since I had book work and receipts to do, we had breakfast at home. We hadn't done this for a long time. It was a beautiful time and all I could think about was how I had asked God, "Should I start a fast today, Lord?" And the answer was always "No."

And Jesus said unto them,
Can the children of the bridechamber fast,
while the bridegroom is with them?
As long as they have the bridegroom with
them, they cannot fast.
But the days will come, when the bridegroom
shall be taken away from them, and then shall
they fast in those days.
(Mark 2:19-20)

A Shame To Speak Of Those Things

Six months after Ken left, I started searching for a Christian counselor. I knew it took two to tango and I also had heard this wise little truism: "He that is convinced against his will is of the same opinion still." I had several men of God to choose from, but God directed me to a counselor who was miles away from me. It took me 30 minutes to get to his office, but for one year, I proceeded to get help with Kevin J. Burnor, M.A., Pastoral Counselor/Pastor.

In this time, I filed for a divorce. I started going to Charlotte Potter's meetings, was teaching Sunday School and began trying to do what Ken had told me to do: "Arlene, get a life."

God then gave me a choice: I could get a divorce or help repair the breach. I chose to stand still and follow God's direction. *"It is good that a man should both hope and quietly wait for the salvation of the Lord"* (Lamentations 3:26). Ken came to me and said, "I don't want a divorce. I want to go to counseling."

I said, "Ok, who do you want to go to?"

He said, "Well, not your counselor!" So I proceeded to get him a counselor. He went several times and then he came to me and said, "I want to go to Kevin." I was shocked, but happy that he really did want help.

I called Kevin (I hadn't talked to him for about six months). I said, "Kevin, how are you?" He said he was fine and then started to laugh as he proceeded to tell me that he knew I was going to call him. I asked him how he knew, and he told me an interesting story.

Kevin had been in a meeting where a prophet named Johnson was, and the prophet said to him, "I hear the name Arlene. I hear the name Arlene."

"I said, 'Well, I had a client named Arlene.' Then the prophet said, 'Well, she's going to call you and you are going to tell her something.'"

I laughed and said, "Well, Kevin, what are you going to tell me?"

Kevin replied, "All I know is that you are doing the right thing."

Ken did go to Kevin for counseling. He's been going for over a year. Many deep roots are being pulled up and discarded. We have been separated almost four years. Ken is coming to the place that God wants for each of His children—the restoration of joy and the presence of God that we're entitled to in our lives. (The joy of the Lord is our strength!)

There were many degrading things in my life that I had to put under my feet, things the Bible says should not be mentioned. I relate back to what Jesus went through on the Cross, the humiliation, the degradation He went through all this to take our sins upon Himself. But, there is no condemnation in His Kingdom!

Proving what is acceptable unto the Lord.
And have no fellowship with the unfruitful works of darkness, but rather reprove them. For it is a shame even to speak of those things which are done of them in secret. But all things that are reproved are made manifest by the light; for whatsoever doth make manifest is light.
(Ephesians 5:10-13)

Cloud of Witnesses

Julie, my daughter, has a girlfriend named Julie. We call her girlfriend Julietta to differentiate between the two. Julietta drew a big picture in church, a picture of the letters J-O-Y. She made the "O" like the sun with rays reaching out from it. She said to my Julie, "This is for your mother because it reminds me of her."

When she brought it to me, I asked her, "Why does this remind you of me, Julietta?"

"Because you're always so joyful."

"Julietta, how can I be always joyful when I'm going through such awful trauma and sadness in my life?"

"But you're not sad, you are very joyful and you make everybody around you joyful," she answered.

This is what I am determined to do. 2 Corinthians 2:1 and 3 says: "But I determined this with myself, that I would not come again to you in heaviness . . . my joy is the joy of you all." This is exactly what I am. Determined. Thank You, Jesus.

*Therefore, since we are surrounded by such
a great cloud of witnesses,
let us throw off everything that hinders
and the sin that so easily entangles, and let us
run with
perseverance the race marked out for us.*
(Hebrews 12:1, NIV)

Mourn Like A Dove

I asked God for a word, saying, "Lord, I'm really hurting." I opened the Word of God and turned to Isaiah 59:11 and began to read. God showed me that when I was beseeching Him in prayer, the sound I was making was the mourning sound of doves. Under this verse was a reference to Isaiah 38:14. I turned back in my Bible and opened the page to Isaiah 38. This Scripture was also about the mourning of doves.

How grateful I was that God was there ministering to me through His Word as I fell asleep.

The next morning I felt I couldn't get up. I said, "Lord, I have to go to the accountant, but I don't think I can do anything." All I could do was lay there for an hour praising the Lord and praying.

Finally I got up and made myself a cup of tea. "Lord, I am not able to do anything today. You will have to do it all." The only thing I was able to do was ask for His help.

Then I heard the words *"the mourning of your supplication . . ."*

"Wait, God, I know what mourning means, but I don't know what supplication means. I've heard enough. I don't want to hear anymore yet." I ran for the dictionary and to my delight found that supplication meant humble prayer or petition to God. He had heard my mourning the night before—like the mourning of doves—and my prayers of petition to Him had been heard.

I flew through my day, blessed and assured. God is and has been in control of my whole life.

> *. . . I did mourn as a dove;*
> *mine eyes fail with looking upward:*
> *O Lord, I am oppressed; undertake for me.*
> **(Isaiah 38:14b)**

Have You Any Right To Be Angry?

For days I would be fine. Then I would see Ken and fall back to lethargy and a feeling of hopelessness. All I could do was go back to bed.

One such day occurred when I was to meet the young man who was going to do the cover for my book. I also had to go to the post office to send off a letter to get permission to use certain materials for this book. As I lay in bed, I said aloud, "Lord, I can't do this." I was alone and began to scream out to God, to praise the Lord and to pray.

I realized that I could again hear the dove mourning in my voice. This got my attention and I said, "Lord, what is wrong?"

I heard, *"A gourd."*

I replied, "A gourd? What do you mean by a gourd? The only gourd I have heard about is the prophet who went out of the city and sat in the shade of a gourd. Then you caused a worm to kill it."

I remembered that the prophet was Jonah and I grabbed my Bible encyclopedia. After attempting to escape his destiny, and spending three days in the belly of a great fish, Jonah finally ended up at Nineveh. Per God's original instructions, he preached again to the wicked and sinful Ninevites as God had called him to do.

When the Ninevites all turned away from their wicked ways and repented, God spared them from the judgment He had made Jonah pronounce on them.

Jonah felt God had made him look foolish so he went out into the countryside and sulked.

God raised up a gourd vine to shade Jonah from the sun, but He allowed a worm to cut it down. Jonah, feeling betrayed again, sighed and complained about the missing plant.

God spoke to Jonah reminding him that He was a God of compassion who had the right to love and forgive anyone who turned to Him in obedience and faith. Jonah had been fretting about his shade plant, but God turned his attention to the worth and salvation of the people of Nineveh.

I began to cry and I asked the Lord to forgive me. I had been angry with Him for not saving Ken's soul when I knew He had the power to do anything. When I asked God to forgive me, He did, and I arose in victory and was soon on my way to complete the requirements of that day.

But the Lord replied, have you any right to be
angry?
(Jonah 4:4, NIV)

I Have Heard Your Prayers

Recently, Julie was at the altar, asking God to give her some answers. She heard God reply to one of her questions and then He said, *"My daughter, your father is coming home."*

When we got home from church that day, there was a note on the door from Ken telling us how much he loved us. Up to that point, Ken had never told the children that he loved me.

I have heard your prayer and seen your tears.
I will heal you.
(2 Kings 20:5, NIV)

The Presence Of The Lord

The Lord showed me in a dream how the angels rejoice when one soul is saved—not the ones who are saved and turn around and go right back out to do their own thing—but how the angels rejoice when a soul is saved who puts God first (Matthew 16:24, 2 Timothy 3:2-5).

We all know the Bible says the angels rejoice, but how? God showed me that if I imagined I had just won a million-dollar lottery or the Kentucky Derby, I might be able to understand their joy.

In my dream, the angels were rejoicing over a soul that was saved (perhaps Ken's). They were wearing pinkish-peach colored, soft-flowing attire. I could only see beauty and a sea of angels. Their voices echoed and the music was so beautiful. When I awoke, all I could remember of the song was the music, but not the words.

I called my daughter, Kimberly, to ask her if she could help me with the title of the song. My son-in-law answered the phone, "Barry, listen, I've got to know the words and the name of this song. I just dreamed the end of the book and I need it." I hummed the whole song to him, but he couldn't help me.

When Kimberly came on the line I explained the whole scenario again and asked her to help me name the song. Her response was, "OK, Mama, let me hear it." I hummed the first two notes and Kimberly instantly said, "Surely the presence of the Lord is in this place." In just two notes, she knew the song. The song tells the senses to see, feel and hear Him—it tells about the manifestation of His presence.

Shortly after this, I went to a large church near my home and saw a young woman who had grown up with Sharon, my baby sister. I was so excited about the dream God had given me that revealed the ending of my book, I said, "Steffie, listen! God has given me the ending of the book in a dream." I shared everything with her and then a few days later, I got a note in the mail from Steffie:

"Hi, Arlene. When you came to Southpoint, you talked to me about the Lord giving you the ending of your book. You hummed part of a song and it stayed in my mind because I really love that song. So, when I ran across this article in a bimonthly magazine, I copied it for you. Enjoy it!"

And I did enjoy it. The article was entitled "*The Story Behind The Song*," the very song the angels were singing in my dream. The article told the story of how the writer of "*Surely the Presence,*" Lanny Wolfe, had received the inspiration for this wonderful song. Here's his story, in his own words:

The Story Behind the Song

It always amazes me how the Lord will give inspiration at times when we don't expect it or at times when we don't ask for it. There was a time in my life when I wanted the Lord to give me a certain number of songs per week. I'd say, "Lord, I'm ready to write today." I had to learn to become workable in His schedule. When He wanted me to have inspiration, He would give it to me. It was my responsibility to be sensitive to the inspiration when it would come. And so it was on a Sunday afternoon at a dedication of a very beautiful church in Mississippi where our Trio was scheduled to sing. Seemingly everybody who was somebody was there; all the things that go with church dedications were in order. As I was sitting there during all the preliminaries in the service, the Lord whispered to me.

Surely the presence of the Lord is in this place.
I can feel His mighty power and His grace.
I can hear the brush of angels' wings.
I see glory on each face.
Surely the presence of the Lord
is in this place.

It came so fast, and the chord progressions that I was hearing in my mind were not the ones I would have normally used. I look back now and wonder how I ever had the boldness to teach this song to Dave, Marietta and the congregation right there on the spot! I started out and the chords and the words came, and the Trio, the musicians and the congregation joined in.

God was in that place because He lives in the fleshly tabernacle of hearts—not because of the stained glass windows or the padded pews or the organ, piano or P.A. set. We need to be reminded of where God lives and that without God's presence, all is in vain. The most beautiful cathedral in the world would be void of His presence if His children were not there, and "Ichabod" could be written on the door. I am glad that God lives within us. He is with us wherever we go; we can meet Him in a brush arbor, at an altar of prayer in a field, under a tree, in our bedroom or in a sanctuary. I am grateful that He has enabled me to be with Him wherever we are.

As His children, *the presence of the Lord* is in us—you and me.

Whatsoever You Bind

You see, Ken came to me on New Year's Day, 1994, and told me again how much he loved me and how he was trying. I told him he couldn't make it just in trying by himself; He also needed God. He said, "I want no one else," he said. "I love you. Please, Arlene, do this my way." I assured him that it must be God's way.

I had never heard of binding and loosing principles until I went to my counselor. I was very leery of such prayers. Yet, I know that the Word says whatsoever is bound on earth will be bound in heaven. I asked the Lord to show me what this Scripture meant.

Then I purchased a copy of the book *Shattering Your Strongholds*© (Bridge-Logos Publishers, New Jersey 1992), which was written by the editor who helped with the editing of my book—Rev. Liberty Savard. As we were wrapping up the final stages of my book, I spoke with her on the phone and she said she felt the Lord wanted me to read and then pray the binding and loosing prayer for others on pages 170-171 in her book. I wrote the pages down and grabbed my copy of her book (which I had not yet read) and prayed the prayer for Ken.

She was having a meeting in her home that night and I wanted to ask her to have the people pray for me, but since I believed it was a Bible study (not a prayer meeting), I decided not to bother her. When I told her this the following week after picking up a final draft of the manuscript, she told me it had been a prayer meeting. I was sorry I had not requested prayer after all, but as I left that day, I asked her if we could pray. She prayed the same prayer for me (from her heart) that I had prayed for Ken from the pages of *Shattering Your Strongholds.*

Later that day I saw Ken and asked him if we could pray together. We knelt at the foot of the bed, like so many times before, and I said, "Lord, here we are again. Have mercy on us. We want nothing else but you. We don't want anything between you and us. We love you, Lord!" Ken also prayed those words and then left.

Right after midnight that evening, New Year's Eve, Ken paged me and I read "7777" on my pager. He didn't want me to call him, just to know he was wishing me a Happy New Year. That was the first time he had ever paged me.

The next evening, Sunday, my pastor asked for testimonies for the New Year. As people were testifying, I got my pager out of my purse to see if I had any calls from the day. I always put it on silent beep when I'm in a service so it won't disturb anyone.

As the testimonies drew to a close, I felt the Spirit of God rising up in me and I had to speak. I stood and said, "Pastor, I want to expound on Isaiah 53. I want everyone to know and realize that nothing is impossible with our God." As I sat down, my pager went off silently in my hand. I looked at it and it said, "708."

I had periodically paged Ken for the past four years (he had no phone during this period of time) and I always put "708" into his pager when I did. Seven meaning completion (for Ken), 0 meaning God circles everything, and 8 meaning me (new beginnings). This was only the second time Ken had ever called me on the pager, but it was the first time he had used "708."

I knew Ken was coming to the place that God wants us to be in our lives. Nothing is impossible to those who believe.

Many waters cannot quench love,
neither can the floods drown it; it a man
would give
all the substance of his house for love,
it would utterly be condemned.
(Song of Solomon 8:7)

With permission from the author and publisher to reproduce here, the following is the anointed prayer that I began praying for Ken on New Year's Day. This prayer can be found in *Shattering Your Strongholds.* (Author: Liberty S. Savard, P.O. Box 41260, Sacramento CA 95841-0260. Publisher: Bridge-Logos Publishers, Florida 1992.)

In the name of Jesus Christ, I bind _____ 's body, soul and spirit to the will and purposes of God for his/her life. I bind _____ 's mind, will and emotions to the will of God. I bind him/her to the truth and to the blood of Jesus. I bind his/her mind to the mind of Christ, that the very thoughts, feelings and purposes of His heart would be within his/her thoughts.

I bind _____ 's feet to the paths of righteousness that his/her steps would be steady and sure. I bind him/her to the work of the cross with all of its mercy, grace, love, forgiveness and dying to self.

I loose every old, wrong, ungodly pattern of thinking, attitude, idea, desire, belief, motivation, habit and behavior from him/her. I tear down, loose any stronghold in his/her life that has been justifying and protecting hard feelings against anyone. I loose the strongholds of unforgiveness, fear and distrust from him/her.

I loose the power and effects of deceptions and

lies from him/her. I loose the confusion and blindness of the god of this world from _____'s mind that has kept him/her from seeing the light of the gospel of Jesus Christ. I call forth every precious word of Scripture that has ever entered in his/her mind and heart that it would rise up in power within him/her.

In the name of Jesus, I loose the power and effects of any harsh or hard words (word curses) spoke to, about or by _____. I loose all generational bondages and associated strongholds from _____. I loose all effects and bondages from him/her that may have been caused by mistakes I have made. Father, in the name of Jesus, I crush, smash and destroy generational bondages of any kind from mistakes made at any point between generations. I destroy them right here, right now. They will not bind and curse any more members of this family.

I bind the strong man, Satan, that I may spoil his house, taking back every material and spiritual possession he has wrongfully taken from _____. I loose the enemy's influence over every part of his/her body, soul and spirit. I loose, crush, smash and destroy every evil device he may try to bring into his/her sphere of influence this day. I bind and loose these things in Jesus' name. He has given me the keys and the authority to do so. Thank You, Lord, for the truth. Amen.

And I will give unto thee the keys of the kingdom of heaven:
and whatsoever thou shalt bind on earth shall be bound in heaven:
and whatsoever thou shalt loose on earth shall be loosed in heaven.
(Matthew 16:19)

Stand Still, And See

After much prayer, I said, "Lord, this night show me what to do." Ken had paged me three times: "708." I was shocked. "Lord, show me something besides standing still. Is it divorce, Lord? Anything you give me to do, I'll act upon it."

I went to bed in deep praise and prayer. Later that night I dreamed in a vision that Ken's mom acquired a beautiful cottage and had it moved onto a lovely piece of land with many trees. Ken and I went to see her and she was busily working on the finishing touches outside the house.

There were some very beautiful green rocks in her yard, nearly twelve inches in diameter. They reminded me of a lovely green glass rock I remembered my grandmother having.

I said, "Mom, wouldn't these be beautiful if they were sliced into stepping stones and placed in a pathway going up to your cottage?" Then I turned to Ken and said, "Ken, if we got one of those knives that cut stone, we could cut these for Mom." He agreed and we left together very happy.

I awoke and remembered what I had asked God and I began to recall the dream in detail. I remember how clear and beautiful the stones were. Then it hit me—Charlotte Potter had prophesied to Ken about those stepping stones being laid.

Ken's mother would see her son change and turn around from what was binding and holding him.

I am to stand still and see the glory of God. He is in complete control.

Fear ye not, stand still, and see the salvation of the Lord . . .

(Exodus 14:13)